CREATIVE
USE OF EMOTION

CREATIVE USE OF EMOTION

BY SWAMI RAMA & SWAMI AJAYA

previously published as
Emotion to Enlightenment

Himalayan International Institute
of Yoga Science and Philosophy of the U.S.A.
Honesdale, Pennsylvania

Himalayan International Institute
of Yoga Science and Philosophy of the U.S.A.
RR 1, Box 400
Honesdale, Pennsylvania 18431

05 04 03 02 01 00 99 98 97 96   8 7 6 5

Library of Congress Cataloging-in-Publication Data
Rama, Swami, 1925 -
        Creative use of emotion.
        Originally published as: Emotion to enlightenment.
        1. Emotions. 2. Self-actualization (Psychology)
3. Yoga. 4. Vedanta. I. Ajaya, Swami, 1940 -
II. Title.
BF531.R29   1986   158'.1   86-223
ISBN 0-89389-093-6

Contents

Introduction

As we expand our awareness, we slowly move from a world of ever-recurring conflicts, discord and suffering, both internally and in our interpersonal relations, to a gradually spreading sense of abiding joy and harmony with all that is. This book is a description of the developmental process which leads to this transformation.

The first chapter sets the scene of the book and provides an overview by describing how consciousness expands. It shows that each individual, as well as mankind as a whole, is growing from a narrow, egocentric point of view toward seeing things from more encompassing perspectives. Each chapter then takes up this theme and shows how it applies to a particular aspect of our functioning. Interwoven with this basic theme are many comparisons between yogic and Vedantic concepts of human development and those of modern psychology.

Chapter Two treats of the development of our self-concept, our sense of identity. It deals with the question, "Who am I?" and the answers put forth at various stages of development. Are there further stages of growth beyond the formation of a stable identity as it has been described in modern psychology? Is one's identity annihilated in the altered states of consciousness described

GOAL: INCREASE YOUR SENSE OF FREEDOM WHILE ACCEPTING GREATER RESPONSIBILITY.

viii   Creative Use of Emotion

THREE:
OTHERS'
INFLUENCE
in the Eastern traditions?   These important questions are dealt with in Chapter Two.

In the third chapter we describe how our self-concept is influenced by innumerable suggestions from others. Because of the many conflicting suggestions coming from outside, we become confused and disoriented. Yoga psychology offers methods for casting off negative suggestions which we have accepted and for learning how to rely on our own direct experience, finally experiencing our own true natures.

FOUR:
This theme is carried forward in Chapter Four which looks at the world as play and drama. We take the drama of life too seriously and identify with the parts we are playing rather than seeking to discover who we are apart from these roles.

FIVE:
Chapter Five discusses the Self, the center of consciousness within. According to yoga and Vedanta psychology, the aim of life and the final stage of development involve
KEY:
disengaging from our false self-concepts and false identifications with the roles and drama to realize our essential nature as the Self.

As we begin to realize our true identities, our interpersonal and family relations and our entire way of living become transformed. As this occurs, there is an increased
GOAL:
sense of freedom accompanied by the acceptance of greater responsibility. Chapter Six shows that freedom and responsibility are in fact interdependent and necessarily develop together.

Emotions and problems arising from them are not clearly understood in modern society. Psychologists have differing opinions about how to deal with our emotional

OPINIONS DIFFER

                                                              versus

life. Some encourage emotional release, while others teach
control or sublimation. Yoga psychology offers a clear,
precise and easily understood conceptualization and
training program in which the energy which gives rise to
such unpleasant emotional states as fear, depression,
jealousy and anger, can be channeled toward the
experience of positive emotional states, such as love,
devotion and bliss. Chapter Seven describes the way in   *SEVEN*
which the various emotions arise from four basic urges
and how this emotional energy finally can be transmuted
and lead us toward enlightenment.

    In the final chapter we trace the development of one
EIGHT: particular emotional attitude, that of judgment and
KEY condemnation, and show how that attitude, which causes
so much suffering both to ourselves and others, is dissolved
as we develop love and forgiveness.

    As we explore the various facets of human life, we see
a lawful development toward increasing harmony and
unity. As we grow, the confusion, uncertainty and mis-
understandings which were once predominant in our
lives are gradually transcended until we finally reach that
state of enlightenment and equilibrium from which all can
be appreciated and understood.

1

The Expansion of Consciousness

This is the Light of all lights, the light of pure Consciousness . . .
lighting up every object in the world, from the sun and stars, from
unconscious mind and conscious reason, to . . . the Omega, and
even the apparent darkness of the *avyakta* [unknown].

The Upanishads

The most abused though well-known words which we
read and hear today are awareness and consciousness.
These words are singular in number, which means there
is only one consciousness or awareness, though on various
levels. We all are aware and conscious of ourselves to some
degree. Even an animal is conscious of itself, like a human
being. But when a human being truly becomes aware
of the existence of others around him, his consciousness
expands and he fulfills the purpose of life.

The more one is conscious of reality as a whole, the
more one becomes aware of the truth which is self-existent
beyond time, space and causation. Consciousness,
awareness and truth are beyond past, present and future.
The human mind is the finest instrument which can be

trained to realize that center from which consciousness
flows in various degrees and grades. However, because their
minds are untrained, most human beings have only a
partial awakening of their consciousness.

Depending   on   individual   characteristics   and
circumstances, a person's consciousness usually has a particular range and focus, with a limited scope. It may be
compared to a small light which illuminates only a tiny
segment of all possible things that may be known. The
light of consciousness radiates in the vast universe, touch-
ing here and there for longer or more brief periods but
never knowing the full design, the meaning and purpose of
what is being touched.

In order to understand this better, imagine the
following situation:

*You are in an immense underground cavern which
extends for many miles in each direction. You are making
your way through this cavern with an oil lamp, trying to
become aware of, and to understand, your circumstances.
The light falls upon a few objects which are close by, and
off in the distance you see some vague shadowy forms.
You are not sure what they are. They remind you of
people and things that you have known before; and you
begin to fantasize, to imagine who and what they may be.*

*Then suddenly the light dies down and you are left
with your memories and imaginings. You grope about in
the darkness for some time and then, after you have
travelled some distance, you are able to turn on the light
again. And again a small area of the immense cavern is
illuminated. Now you see something quite different*

from what you had seen before. Some new forms are seen distinctly and others in the distance are barely made out. Some of them are pleasing and beautiful, others may be repugnant. But soon the light goes out once more, and you are left with another piece of a jigsaw puzzle, not quite knowing how it may fit with those which you have collected until now.

As you travel about in this way you come across many interesting experiences, many enchanting sights. You begin to believe that by accumulating a vast number of such experiences your awareness and comprehension of the entire cavern will grow.

Many of us go through life in a similar way. We think that expanded awareness means accumulating as great a variety of experiences as possible within our lifetime. We wander about aimlessly in one direction and then in another, seeking to have as many adventures as possible. But after we have travelled through the uncountable variety of lands, homes, jobs, encounters, relationships and projects that life has to offer, we remain puzzled as to why it all happened. All too often in this journey of life we come to the end looking back and wondering what it was all about.

Let us return to our experience in the cavern:

Imagine now that you have learned to regulate the lamp in such a way that the light does not go out. As you adjust it and turn it up, you begin to see better. The objects in the distance, which were previously seen only vaguely, become clear and are sharply distinguished.

*As the light grows even brighter and more intense, the
entire cavern becomes illuminated and you are able to walk
about observing all that it contains. Everything can now
be known and understood.*

The growth of consciousness does not consist of
travelling about with an uncertain light that illuminates a
series of random fields in the vast unknown. Instead, it
is the steady and systematic expansion of one's range of
vision so that more and more may be taken in, until finally
the field of awareness extends to include all and nothing
remains outside it. The expansion of consciousness does
not lie in the quantitative accumulation of experiences,
but in a qualitative change in the person experiencing.
The path of development, be it the development of an
individual or of mankind as a whole, may best be charac-
terized and understood at its core as a gradual and
progressive expansion of awareness. Understanding the way
in which consciousness grows and the laws which govern
its growth can provide us with meaning and guidance for
our lives. Having an overview of this growth process can
help us to understand the characteristics and qualities of
a limited consciousness, and those of a consciousness
which is more developed. If we can discern a general
pattern in the development of consciousness, we may
begin to understand where we are along this path and
to gain some knowledge of the landmarks that lie ahead
of us. We will then have a map to guide us so that we
may progress directly and efficiently instead of being
caught up in the experiences acquired at any particular
level of illumination. This book will explore the way in

which one's thinking, feelings, attitudes and self-concept are systematically transformed as consciousness is expanded.

A New Perspective

One of the major changes which occurs as consciousness expands is a movement from a limited, narrow and exclusive perspective to one which is more comprehensive and inclusive. When the light of consciousness is small, whatever is not included in its boundaries is alien. Thus an individual whose consciousness is not well developed will tend to look at the world from an egocentric perspective and will be unable to appreciate the concerns and viewpoints of others. There will be considerable conflict in this person's life as he relates to people in his environment.

The lack of harmony and integration that such a person experiences with respect to the external environment is also characteristic of the internal environment of his own mind. When consciousness is not well developed, the unconscious remains relatively vast. Thoughts, desires and self-concepts tend to be fragmented and are often at odds with one another. They are perceived vaguely and remain uncoordinated and uncontrolled. Such lack of harmony within ourselves as well as between ourselves and our environment leads to considerable emotional instability, fears, anxieties, and a life filled with turmoil and confusion. But as consciousness expands, a process of integration takes place among all the alienated or conflicting aspects of ourselves. As the light of awareness becomes brighter, we begin to see the natural order inherent inside and outside

of us, and this new understanding brings increased
happiness and satisfaction.

Let us now work with another illustration:

*Imagine that you are lost in a deep valley, surrounded
by thickly growing bushes and trees. You are only able to
see a short distance ahead and on the sides, because of the
dense forest surrounding you. You are preoccupied with
protecting yourself and satisfying your immediate needs.
You are concerned with finding water, food, shelter, and
protection from animals. You feel frightened and
desperate, wondering how you will ever find your way
out.*

*After a considerable struggle you finally climb to the
top of the ridge surrounding the valley. There your
field of awareness is extended and you can look down to
the spot where you were previously standing. From this
higher vantage point you see a winding stream, and some
fruit trees just a short distance off from where you had
been. When you were in the valley the water and trees
were unknown. For you, they did not exist. The fear of
suffering from thirst and hunger was very real to you then.
But from your larger perspective at the top of the ridge
you can see that there was no need to be concerned at
all. Your problems were created by your own imagination,
by the narrowness of your perception.*

*From the ridge where you are now standing you can
see even higher plateaus surrounding you, and you wonder
what lies beyond them. Though your perspective is
greater than it was before, it is still far from all-
encompassing. You are still preoccupied with finding your*

way out of the wilderness and seeking shelter.

Though your field of vision has been enlarged and your anxieties somewhat reduced, many uncertainties remain. So you begin to make your way toward a higher vantage point. It takes considerable time and effort to reach it, but when you finally climb, exhausted, to the top of a large hill, your efforts are rewarded by a still greater perspective and you are overjoyed to see in the distance a trail and beyond it, still further, the smoke and tents of some campers.

Each time you climb to a higher vantage point the range of your vision is enlarged and your understanding of your entire situation is altered. You see things from a more encompassing perspective which allows you to be less concerned and anxious and enables you to relate to your environment in terms of how it really is rather than in terms of how you imagined it to be from a more limited point of view.

The entire process of human development may be understood as a process of broadening our perspective. If we look at the history of our civilization or if we study the way a child develops, we will see a pattern in which our frame of reference is gradually extended. Initially the range of vision is curtailed and there is an egocentric orientation. The world is seen in terms of the perceiver being at the center of the universe. But gradually, as consciousness expands, we become less self-centered, less preoccupied with trivial individual concerns, and are thus able to view a wider range of phenomena.

Numerous examples of how consciousness evolves

along this continuum can be found in the history of Western science. For example, there was a time when man thought that the earth was the center of the universe and that the sun, planets and stars revolved around this center. Anyone who thought differently was considered a heretic. Then, with the Copernican revolution, man became aware that the planets, the sun and stars do not revolve around the earth, but that in fact the earth moves around the sun. More recently, as our perspective has become even less egocentric, we have realized that our own solar system is just a small part of a vast galaxy which itself is only one amongst countless others. As our knowledge of the universe becomes more clear, we find ourselves no longer believing we are the center of all. We have a more objective understanding of how each aspect of the universe, including ourselves, is interrelated with others.

In other areas of science there has been a similar development toward a larger frame of reference. Einstein's concept of relativity goes far beyond the man-centered Newtonian scheme and requires us to be able to conceive of the world from frames of reference other than our own. In the biological and psychological sciences too, there has been a movement away from an anthropocentric orientation. Darwin and Lamarck challenged the traditional belief in man's uniqueness and dominion over other living creatures by placing him in the context of evolutionary development. Similarly, Freud helped to undermine the commonly held notion that man is a wholly rational being with full control over his decisions and actions. In each of these areas, as our knowledge has grown, the idea that man's "I" is at the center and in control of his universe has been replaced by a larger viewpoint which more realistically enables man to see how he fits into his environment.

If we consider the history of art, we also see an increasing awareness and appreciation of multiple perspectives. Early artistic creations showed little or no sense of perspective. The world was portrayed in a flat, two-dimensional manner. But as painting developed, the mastery of perspective was achieved. Today artists such as Picasso no longer confine their painting to a single point of view, but present their subject from multiple perspectives. They show us that there are alternative and equally valid ways to experience the same situation.

If we turn to look at the growth of the individual, we will see a similar pattern. Jean Piaget, one of the foremost developmental psychologists, has described the growth process as a movement away from egocentrism. In summarizing Piaget's viewpoint, one psychologist states:

> The infant believes that the existence of physical objects is contingent upon his motor activity or his perception. Only at the end of this stage does he undergo a miniature "Copernican revolution" and conceive of himself as merely one entity in the universe of permanent objects.
>
> Egocentrism marks the child's early transactions with the social world as well. . . . He cannot conceive of other persons holding viewpoints different from his own. . . .
>
> Piaget claims that a child is about seven years of age before he is capable of having a true discussion with other children, thereby indicating that he has grasped the idea that there are other points of view.*

* Charles Wenar, *Personality Development*, Houghton Mifflin, Boston, 1974, p. 194.

Thus in the history of science as well as in art and in the course of an individual's personal development we can see a common trend leading away from the single self-centered vantage point toward greater flexibility, in which different approaches may even be taken simultaneously. This growth process leads us away from conflict and dissension toward integration and harmony.

When we study the lives of great people or those who are considered to be creative and dynamic in the world we find certain common characteristics. There is a movement from individuality to universality. But we find this expansion of consciousness occurring in two ways. The sages and the spiritual leaders expanded their consciousness by fathoming the grosser levels, going toward the subtler levels of their own being, and finally coming to that subtlest center of consciousness which is the *summum bonum* of the life force. This way of expansion is purely spiritual and is found in the lives of those like Jesus, Moses, Krishna and Buddha. There is another way of expanding consciousness which is found among scientists like Newton and Einstein, artists like Van Gogh and Picasso, and poets such as Keats, Shelley, Longfellow and Wordsworth. Their creative and dynamic way of expanding consciousness was external. We find two classes of great men, one studying the gross world of manifestation, searching, experimenting and coming out with certain conclusions. The other goes to more and more subtle realms of awareness. The purpose of their search is to find the underlying unity in the apparent diversity.

2

The Transformation of Identity

Yoga is the control of the thought-waves in the mind.
Then man abides in his real nature.
At other times, when he is not in the state of yoga, man remains
identified with the thought-waves in the mind.

Patanjali

We typically identify ourselves with the objects of
our thoughts and thus assume that we are joyous or
miserable. But when awareness expands and we start
establishing ourselves in our true nature, the center of
consciousness within us, we find that we can rise above
all pains and pleasures. Fortunate are the few who
establish themselves in their true nature.

When we come into the world as an infant, our
consciousness is open to the new environment. We have
not yet formed ways of organizing our perceptions and do
not know who or what we are. We reach out looking
around for some order, some recognition of what the
multicolored chaos is all about. The lack of filtering
and organizing make for a great deal of uncertainty, and

from the very beginning we attempt to find a basis of stability. We gradually start building boundaries around ourselves to establish our individuality, and the darkness of our ignorance obscures the vision of our totality, our universal life. For instance, a wave in the ocean is not actually separate from the ocean even though it seems to form its own individual nature and is called by its own individual name. From childhood onward we are taught to develop a sense of individuality, and we remain on the level of names and forms, never aware of the underlying unity. We start discriminating between what is I and what is not I without knowing the totality of the self. Each of the things in the world apparently has a separate identity. But when we go to the source we find that in reality there is only one unity. Between these two extremes lies the confusion of identifying ourselves with the objects of the world, and we normally do not find a way to transcend the world of identification.

As we grow up our self-definition becomes more and more clearly outlined and we begin to form what might be called an identity. Modern psychologists who study the growth process suggest that the time of adolescence is especially significant in the formation of an identity. Erik Erikson suggested that the "adolescent identity crisis" is resolved when we firmly establish a career, home, family and life-style of our own.

When Erikson first described the development of identity a generation ago, the formation of a stable self-image was seen as the ultimate goal. A reluctance to find a niche in life was viewed as retarded, regressive or even pathological. A person who would not settle down to a permanent job and family was considered aimless and irresponsible at best, and severely disturbed at worst. Arthur Miller's character, Biff, in *Death of a Salesman*, provides an example of an adult who psychologically remains at the adolescent stage of development and is unable to establish a solid identity. Biff says:

> I've had twenty or thirty different kinds of jobs since I left home. . . . I . . . get the feeling . . . I'm not getting anywhere! . . . I'm thirty-four years old, I oughta be makin' my future. . . .
> I'm mixed up very bad. Maybe I oughta get married. Maybe I oughta get stuck into something. Maybe that's my trouble. I'm just a boy. I'm not married, I'm not in business, . . . I'm like a boy.*

Miller vividly portrays one of the major difficulties in the formation of identity: the inability to progress beyond the uncertainty of adolescence, to take a stance, and to make a commitment to a particular life-style. But there is another pathological syndrome which may be understood as the opposite extreme. There are also people who take such a firm hold of a particular self-concept and life-style, clinging tenaciously and compulsively to the identity they have established, that there remains practically no possibility for further growth.

As our self-concept becomes more and more clearly defined, that which lies outside of ourself is also more clearly delineated. We live in a world of duality which consists of that which is "me and mine" and that which

---

* Arthur Miller, *Death of a Salesman*, Viking Press, New York, 1949, pp. 22-23.

is not. The limited self-definition which we create for
ourselves has a useful purpose, for it enables us to function
in a coordinated manner. Without having a sense of our
distinctness from the rest of the world, it would be
extremely difficult to provide for ourselves and to take
care of everyday existence. Limiting our self-definition
makes the world manageable for us. Yet it also creates
for us a sense of separation from all that we define as
"not I."   And this separation, this duality, creates
discomfort, disharmony, and at times even a feeling of
loneliness and isolation.

We have learned to guide ourselves and to control
our situation through developing a concept of ourselves
as distinct individuals. But this distinction leads us to
feel incomplete, and there is a basic urge in us to transcend
our present state. A great deal of our time and effort is
directed toward establishing relationships with what is
experienced as the "not I," and here lies the essential
dilemma of our life. We are at a pivotal point in the
evolution of consciousness: we have created for ourselves
a self-concept which excludes the rest of the world, an
artificial sense of separation which has its practical
benefits. But at the same time we suffer from pangs of
isolation and desperately seek to re-establish unity.

Erich Fromm has suggested that the search for unity
is the basic motivation in man:

> The experience of separateness arouses anxiety; it is indeed
> the source of all anxiety. . . .
> The deepest need in man, then, is the need to overcome his
> separateness, to leave the prison of his aloneness. . . .
> Man—of all ages and cultures— is confronted with the solution

to one and the same question: the question of how to overcome separateness, how to achieve union, how to transcend one's own individual life and find at-onement.*

The wish to transcend our separation and find union can be seen in a great many of our everyday activities. Our use of hallucinogenic drugs, alcohol and other intoxicants, sexual encounters, the thrill of a roller coaster ride, or driving at high speeds may be seen as examples of our strong desire to lose ourselves in the moment, to cast off our sense of separateness and to experience merging, however temporary and partial it may be.

But the person who has developed too strong a self-concept, too much of a sense of separate identity, holding onto it fiercely and compulsively, finds considerable difficulty in achieving any degree of genuine self-transcendence. Even his sexual experiences will feel unsatisfying as he finds himself unable to "let go." Such a person may seek out false substitute ways of getting beyond himself. He may believe he can transcend his small isolated "I" by acquiring many possessions which may be brought within the realm of his control and within his self-definition. As he gains a house, family, car, speedboat and other possessions which may be called "mine," he may feel as if his "I" has been enlarged and his sense of isolation diminished. The more he acquires, the greater control he seems to have over his world. Outwardly it might appear that he has indeed overcome his isolation when he has many people working under his direction,

* Erich Fromm, *The Art of Loving*, Harper & Bros., New York, 1956, pp. 8-9.

serving him or seeking to please him. However, in the long run such an individual is likely to find out that the loneliness is not reduced at all but that his alienation may actually become greater.

Some people have such highly developed abilities for extending their territories through the acquisition of wealth, prestige or power over others that they may rise to important positions, using their organizational skills to run corporations, governments, and other institutions. Identifying with their enterprises they may augment their self-concept to enormous proportions and yet find that their sense of completeness does not increase. For such people their very strength is their weakness, and their feeling of being distinct from others is especially acute. Outward success, the enlargement of position and possessions, may actually create a barrier to any real self-development and self-transcendence. For success often leads to clinging more tenaciously to one's established image. Only the external appearance of identity growth is there. One may delude oneself with a false sense of security and with the feeling that he has overcome his isolation. But in reality one is merely collecting people and objects which, however closely they may be drawn to his bosom, cannot become part of him nor he a part of them.

The Expansion of Identity

Are there any alternatives to the state of alienation produced by a rigid identity? Once we have established a particular self-concept and life-style, what else can we do but cling to our basis of security more tenaciously when beset by feelings of loneliness, anxiety and fear? How can we think about changing our identity so that it might become more inclusive? Wouldn't letting go of the way we have done things and looked at things for all these years be a kind of regression to a pre-adolescent stage? We certainly do not want to be like Biff, trying one thing and another and never settling down into a stable way of life. And yet what other choices are there?

These questions have not been fully answered by modern psychology, which has not yet offered us an adequate understanding of how to achieve growth beyond the formation of a fixed identity and life-style. A clear distinction has not been made between a fragmented, underdeveloped sense of identity and the purposeful process of transcending our narrow identity, which may involve passing through a temporary state of confusion and then developing a more inclusive transcending self-concept. All too often the confusion that comes with dissolving an unsatisfactory identity is viewed as a pathological rather than a constructive and beneficial development.

Modern psychology has emphasized the study of how we build permanent identities. Personality is considered to be the cornerstone of our self-concept, and the establishment of stable, lasting personality types has been thought to be important. By contrast, Eastern psychology focuses on the ongoing process of discovering new and broader identities, with uncovering misconceptions about the nature of our being and letting go of those misconceptions to attain a more encompassing point of view.

Moreover, modern psychology has emphasized the growth process through the stage of identity formation, and until very recently has given little attention to developmental processes which can occur beyond this stage. But some psychologists have suggested that there are more evolved stages in the growth process, although they are attained by relatively few individuals. Psychologists recognize that a person may become partially entrenched in an early stage of development so that he does not mature properly. Biff is an example of someone caught up in the adolescent stage and unable to progress to adult identity formation. If there are further stages in the growth process, could it be that the majority of people in today's culture are entrenched in the firm identity they developed in early adulthood, and do not even know about progress to stages beyond?

It is natural for psychologists, in theorizing about the pattern of development, to reflect the qualities of the people they study. If we are to develop a psychology which envisions further stages in the growth process, it might be necessary to study individuals who are functioning at more evolved levels. However, most of our psychological theories are based on the study of the "typical" person, or on those who are psychologically disturbed.

Those who have studied "self-actualized," gifted, or more conscious individuals suggest that there are indeed further stages in development. Maslow's theory of Self-Actualization, Bucke's descriptions of Cosmic Consciousness, and concepts being developed by the transpersonal psychologists all point out that there are further stages in the growth process. They suggest that more evolved stages of development involve less self-preoccupation and more concern for others. There seems to be an expansion of the field of interest as we pass beyond the stage of identity formation. Erikson hints at this when he says:

> The young adult, emerging from the search for and insistence on identity, is eager and willing to fuse his identity with that of others. He is ready for intimacy, that is, the capacity to commit himself to concrete affiliations and partnerships.*

While Western psychology is just beginning to explore the possibility of more evolved stages of growth, yoga psychology has long ago emphasized this level of development. Modern psychotherapy can assist us in completing the earlier development from a confused and uncertain identity to a solid identity based on the principle of separation. But yoga psychology can take us further and help us transcend constricting identities to achieve a more encompassing awareness of who and what we are, and finally establish ourselves in our true nature which is peace, happiness and bliss.

In exploring the expanded identity, yoga psychology teaches that letting go of a self-concept which has caused pain, conflict and anxiety need not necessarily lead to the regressive uncertainty about who we are that often characterizes adolescence. It is possible instead to replace an older, constricting identity with a new one which is more embracing and more inclusive of what has previously

---

* Erik H. Erikson, *Childhood and Society,* W. W. Norton, New York, 1963, p. 263.

been defined as "not I." We can let go of our grip on an exclusive self-definition which produces a great deal of loneliness, while at the same time we take a foothold in another larger self-definition. This experience of giving up some aspect of our narrow sense of identity and replacing it with a broader one can be an exhilarating event. When this happens in our life, even in a minor way, there is a feeling of openness and lightness, a sense of freshness and ease that are the true signs of overcoming isolation.

Many Western psychologists have erroneously interpreted Eastern explanations of transcendent consciousness as involving a loss of the ego, as if all sense of individuality and uniqueness were to be left behind in some sort of complete merging involving a total loss of "I." To most people such a fantasized loss of their identity is frightening. But in actuality this does not occur, for the evolution of consciousness is not an annihilation but an expansion of identity. This expansion takes place not through self-aggrandizement but through gradual self-redefinition. In this process we need not fear that our identity will be lost for it is ever with us.

It is often said in mystical writings that the ego dies with the awakening of higher consciousness. But the word *ego* is often not properly understood. Ego is a concept that has a rather broad range of definition in its normal usage. In modern psychology the word ego is used primarily to describe an aspect of the mind which is responsible for coordinating mental functioning. It is the thinking, reasoning, evaluative aspect of the mind. Ego is the computer which weighs, sorts and calculates.

But there is another entirely different concept of ego. In our everyday language ego means an extreme amount of self-interest to the exclusion and detriment of others. When we use such terms as "egotistical" we refer to people who have a "strong ego" with a negative connotation. However, a psychologist in talking about someone with a well-developed ego is describing a person who has considerable coping skills and can deal effectively with the environment. There is no implication that such skills need go along with an egotistical type of personality.

When we hear that in higher states of consciousness the ego is dissolved, this refers only to the word "ego" that is used to denote narrow self-interest and lack of concern for other people or for our environment. It does not at all imply a diminution of the coordinating and cognitive abilities of the ego. The expanded identity contains all of the essential capacities of thinking, reasoning, logical analysis, the ability to filter out sensory inputs, to plan ahead and to use past experiences—in short, it includes all of the positive qualities of the ego which develop in normal adulthood and allow us to cope effectively with our environment.

As consciousness grows, we give up limited self-concepts and open ourselves to new, more encompassing ways of defining ourselves. We become less preoccupied with the small "I" that lives within the confines of our physical body. Instead we begin to acquire a definition of ourselves which extends beyond this narrow framework. Old identities are given up, but the coordinating capacities of the ego remain and are used in the service of new and larger identities. Our basic sense of "I" is not lost but simply undergoes a slow process of transformation.

Such an expanded identity enables us to live and function in the world in a much more integrated and meaningful way than before. For instance, a typically narrow sense of identity might lead us to look at the world from this viewpoint: "This hand is part of me. I'd better not injure it or I'll be hurting myself. But that hand over there belongs to someone else; it isn't part of me. If it gets injured I won't suffer. I don't have to take care of that hand. . . ." There's a clear distinction here between the narrow sense of oneself and the estranged world outside. But as our identity expands we come to a greater awareness of the way in which all beings are interrelated. For example, we may become aware that an injury that we do to someone else may actually have an effect on ourselves. With a limited self-concept we might not be concerned with polluting the environment. We might toss empty pop cans about the park during a picnic when no one is looking. We might break the limb off a tree with the attitude, "It doesn't affect me, I'll just get away with whatever I can." But as our self-concept becomes more inclusive, we begin to see that what we do to the external environment comes back to us. We find, for example, that the park with the accumulated litter no longer offers us pleasant recreation.

As our awareness grows we take in a larger field of concern and responsibility. Our sense of separation between ourselves and others becomes less and less acute. From the perspective of an expanded identity we find that we are all part of a larger organism functioning as a whole. In our physical body each individual cell works as part of the total structure and may even sacrifice itself for the general welfare. An expanded identity helps us organize our lives on a similar basis, to begin to work for the common benefit, for "all of us" rather than for "me and mine." There is a new sense of harmony with all of life which was absent when our self-concept was more narrow. We gradually outgrow our sense of isolation and come to realize that the isolation which we felt was not a real and objective quality of life but a misconception, an illusion based on the way we organized our experience.

The expansion of identity is best described not as a process of accumulating or adding on to ourselves but rather as learning to give up and let go. Paradoxically, we find that our understanding and our self-concept are enhanced through letting go of our old viewpoint. In order to grow we must give up the narrow self-definition we have built up. When we let go of our grip on a narrow self-definition we find a more open and inclusive self-concept in its place.

Redefining ourselves more broadly is the only productive way in which isolation can be left behind. All attempts to overcome separateness by extending ourselves through domination and accumulation are in vain. Even those areas of life which are traditionally recognized as leading to self-transcendence will lose their value if approached with a self-seeking attitude. For example, falling in love with another or becoming involved in a spiritual quest will turn into a mere mimicry of the real experience, if we are motivated by the desire for self-aggrandizement.

The more narrow and more rigidly held is one's concept

of identity, the more insecure he will be, feeling small in the world which seems large and threatening. The person with the narrow identity works primarily to achieve security, and his chief concern is with what he can obtain for self-protection. But as consciousness expands there is a movement from this egocentric orientation toward greater openness and integration. Instead of acting from a sense of isolation and insecurity, he begins to act from a sense of fullness and interrelatedness. He is no longer so concerned with what he might derive from other people and from the environment, for he can see the intimate link between himself and all.

A person with a narrow separatist identity does not see the larger pattern of his life. In giving, he feels that some part of him is being lost and must be replaced with something in return. But the person with a more expanded identity, in giving is not worried about getting back his due. Instead of looking at himself as an isolated being struggling against the rest of the world, he views himself as intimately connected with the whole and working for the greater benefit of the whole. He sees himself as one cell in the large body of humanity. The idea of working and living only for himself, for what he can draw from others, seems absurd.

Just as the physical body could not function if each organ and cell worked only for itself, the coordination of our lives together could not proceed unless we worked for the common good. If one part of our physical body desired to be ascendant over the rest of our body, an internal conflict would result, leading to trouble and disease. Similarly, if individuals work only for their own aggrandizement, the rest of the body of humanity suffers and conflict and war are the inevitable results. A person with an expanded identity thoroughly understands this and lives his life in such a way as to prevent discord and to create harmony within and around him.

How Yoga Psychology Approaches the Transformation of Identity

Yoga psychology, in leading us toward expanded consciousness, focuses considerable attention on how the firm identity which we struggled so long to build up is to be dismantled piece by piece. As we evolve, all of those constructs that defined the world in terms of "me and mine" must slowly be abandoned and replaced. In this process the student first turns his attention to his gross identifications with externals. He seeks to understand the way in which he has identified with his possessions, family, social stratum, other people, and objects. He looks at the way in which such identifications lead to conflicts and unhappiness, and through the practice of meditation gradually loosens his hold on all these things in establishing his self-image.

As he progresses, he begins to investigate those identifications which occur inwardly, in his thoughts. The process of work in yoga is a movement from the grosser, external, and more obvious to the more inward and subtle, which is unusual and contrary to the teachings and training that are imparted to us in the world. Usually we get only one aspect of teaching and training. The Reality still remains in the unknown. When we become aware of this process which leads us from the gross to subtler and then to the most subtle aspects of our being, then we no longer identify ourself with the objects but with our own essential nature.

As the aspirant becomes more aware of the inner workings of his mind, he gradually begins to dissociate himself from mental images, suggestions, symbols, ideas, fancies and fantasies which remain latent in his unconscious. He learns to observe these thoughts objectively, watching how they come before his mind almost as though they belonged to another person. From this neutral perspective he learns little by little to keep himself from becoming caught up and taken in by those thoughts which are unproductive or harmful. Instead of identifying with them, as had been the case before he started meditation, the student merely observes the parade of ideas and impressions in his mind. Slowly, through this process of observation, he comes to realize that he is someone other than who he thought he was.

Thus the groundwork is laid for a new identity. It is only when involvement with those thoughts that comprised one's old self-concept is weakened and eventually eliminated that one is freed from the old identity. As this happens, other self-concepts may gradually be formed. At first one may be unaware of them, but as the practice of meditation continues, they will surface into awareness. If one is to continue to grow, they too must be given up. As this process goes on, one's self-concept slowly becomes broader and broader, more and more inclusive.

Patanjali, the codifier of yoga psychology, suggests

that when we identify with the train of thought patterns, we are subject to confusion and restlessness, forgetting our true nature and identifying ourselves with the objects of the mind. These thoughts lead us hither and thither without any aim. According to Patanjali, when consciousness does not tie itself to any thoughts, it remains in a state of equanimity where all is peaceful and filled with perennial joy and eternal compassion.

The main point of yoga psychology is to understand that the center of self-consciousness is different from the thought patterns. This is a notion that at first may seem alien to Westerners raised on the Cartesian dictum, "I think, therefore I am." In defining ourselves, we believe that the thoughts which come before our mind are an essential part of us. If we were to try and distinguish ourselves from them, we would be left in a quandary. We might ask ourselves, "If I am not my thoughts, then what could I possibly be? Is there anything left?" Modern psychology would tend to answer that question negatively, for it does not make a real distinction between an individual and his mental process. But yoga psychology teaches that consciousness can exist apart from our thoughts, thoughts being merely the instruments of consciousness. Those who have experienced states of pure consciousness describe them as unfettered and limitless states of harmony, wisdom and bliss which transcend thoughts as we know them. The inward method for knowing our true identity is not subject to discussion, clarification or argument, but is subject only to practical experience.

Yoga psychology teaches a way of giving up even the

most subtle aspects of our limiting identifications. The various practices of yoga bring about the gradual erasure of our belief that we are those ideas, worries, confusions, hopes, fears and dependencies that continuously occupy our mind. Different yogic methods, working together or independently, are all aimed at teaching us to surrender identifications, to reduce our attachment to externals, and to live in harmony with others rather than spending our time and energy enhancing our narrow sense of "I." The teachings of yoga bring the student again and again before his own reflection, helping him to shed his false identities one after another. This process eventually brings the student to the realization that there is something in him which underlies all transitory images of the "I."

One of the well-known paths in yoga for achieving this realization is called Jnana Yoga, or the yoga of knowledge. In this approach, the student is taught directly the wisdom which comes about indirectly through other yogic practices. In Jnana Yoga the student confronts his false identifications through his intellect. We can see how this approach works with the concept of identity when we examine one of its variations.

In the method of self-query the student sits in meditation, emptying his mind of all thoughts. When a thought arises, he immediately asks himself, "Who am I? Am I this thought?" He concludes, "No, I am not. This thought is coming before me and I am observing it, but I am not the thought and am not affected by it." Many thoughts may come before the mind of the meditator. For example, he may remember an experience which frightened him. However, instead of re-experiencing the fright, with the corresponding physiological and psychological discomforts that the memory arouses, he will look at the whole thing as a neutral observer. He will let it pass by. One by one, the many potentially unsettling thoughts that arise in the mind are neutralized, as again and again the student says, "Who am I? No, I am not this thought. I am something beyond this thought." Eventually he develops a sense of serenity, peace and joy as his identity is disengaged from the mental turbulence.

In another variation of this method, the student may deliberately ask himself, "Who am I?" Whatever thought comes to his mind as an answer is looked at and then rejected. Then the question is asked again, another answer comes and it too is discarded. Gradually the student moves from more superficial answers based on external factors to more subtle ones. But he discards even these and continues the query. At this point, aspects of his self-concept that were formerly at an unconscious level may come into his awareness. The student can examine them and realize the way his unconscious is influencing him. He will ultimately understand that he is not any of the things that he had imagined himself to be. He is something beyond all of his previous self-concepts. As this awareness grows, he becomes more and more open to the immediate experience of the present moment without limiting himself to any preconceptions of who and what he is. Through this process the student transcends the confines of the way in which he had programmed his mind into the categories "I" and "not I."

Learning how to give up identifications freely and to continually open ourselves to consciousness growth is a slow and laborious process. It may take many years and uncountable lessons, requiring many patient hours from teachers, counselors and friends to see us through this journey. One might compare this process to the birth of a child. Yoga psychology acts much as a midwife in assisting the delivery. It teaches a practice which might be analogous to natural and non-violent childbirth, in which the experience is transformed from pain and fear to inspiration and joy.

𝕐 3

From Suggestion to Direct Experience

Those who love the Truth in each thing are to be called lovers of wisdom and not lovers of opinion.

Plato

Life is learning and the usual way of learning known by humanity so far is through suggestion. When a child grows and starts learning he learns through the suggestions of his parents, brothers, sisters, friends, neighbors and anyone who comes in contact with him. Suggestion seems to be the most influential means of acquiring beliefs and opinions about ourselves, others and the world in which we live. But the experiences which we receive through suggestion are not unalloyed experiences and do not satisfy the inner being. For suggestion merely provides indirect experiences which we accept from our environment and educational institutions. These are important in communicating with the world but are not completely fulfilling as far as the aim of life is concerned. So often we want to see, know, hear and understand more. We discuss, argue, think and often reject suggestions from others so that we can find out directly for ourselves.

When the mind, intellect and ego do not have direct experience they do not become competent instruments for attaining higher knowledge, an individual does not become aware of the reality outside the boundaries of his mind. Direct experience is beyond all doubts and satisfies human curiosity, intuition and the search for knowledge. There is definitely a higher source of knowledge which comes through direct experience. The knowledge which dawns through such direct experience is called unalloyed knowledge to which all human beings aspire.

Suggestions can be positive or negative. Negative suggestions leave one disheartened and cripple the whole process of learning. A clear example of the influence of negative suggestions can be found in the *Bhagavad Gita.* Sanjaya, the messenger of the opposing army, gave Arjuna negative suggestions and he started shivering with fear. Negative suggestions can be so powerful and influential that even a warrior like Arjuna could lose his discrimination. Such negative suggestions are definitely a part of learning and are always at the root of mentally deranged and imbalanced people.

There are two varieties of suggestion. One is auto-suggestion and another is suggestion from others. The founders of psychology, psychoanalysis, and psycho-therapy in the West, such as Charcot, Adler, James, Freud and several others, found that suggestion could be useful, but in some cases only up to a certain extent. That is why their research changed its direction toward other methods of therapy. Positive auto-suggestions or positive suggestions received from others definitely inspire and help but they cannot lead one toward direct experience, which is the quest of the human mind and heart.

How Suggestions Influence Us

Suggestions of various sorts begin to influence us from the very moment of our birth and continue almost uninterruptedly from all corners for a long time, pulling us in one direction and then in another, and leading us off into different worlds of experience.

Suggestions begin to influence us from our first waking moment of each day. *If you wake up in the morning to a clock-radio the first thing you may hear is the news, "Seven persons were killed in a guerilla attack. . . . War is expected to erupt in . . . ." Or it might be some wistful music; a young man sings of his lost love. This is followed by an advertisement telling you not to miss a new movie that will excite and frighten you beyond anything you have ever experienced. When you get out of bed, the person you are living with adds further suggestions. Perhaps he or she will tell you how wonderful you look or how awful, or warn you of walking barefoot and catching cold. Later, you dress and catch your ride for work. The car radio is on and you hear the suggestion, "Drink . . . It will make you young and livelier." The song that comes on next gives you further suggestions about how to think and feel about yourself and about others. At noon someone suggests that you go out and have a big meal together. You know it's not good for you because you're overweight, but it appears so tempting that you give in.*

Later your friend tells you about a wonderful movie she has just seen (the same one you heard about earlier on the radio), so that evening you decide to go and see it.

And so it continues. All day you are exposed to a stream of suggestions of all sorts and varieties, often contradictory. They come not only from the radio and TV, but from billboards, magazines, newspapers, friends and acquaintances. Everyone with whom we interact gives us suggestions, intentionally or not, often in subtle non-verbal ways. These many and variegated suggestions often lead us toward chaos, confusion and uncertainty. Many things come before us with the cumulative effect of creating considerable turmoil and unrest.

As we act on these suggestions, our actions also become disorganized. *A friend urges you to read a new book so you rush down to the store to get it. But on the way you see a sign in a store announcing a sale. You become distracted and stop there, in your haste forgetting to put a nickel in the parking meter so that when you come out you have a parking ticket. Momentarily you are upset but you hurry on to the many tasks and activities that you have planned, to follow up on the many suggestions that have come your way.*

Most of us are not really aware of the extent to which suggestions affect us. Even when we become aware of this, we fail to realize that we can increase our ability to sort out and select only certain suggestions to follow. Many of us take the attitude that chaos and confusion are just a part of the way life is. But if we understand the tremendous power of suggestion, then we may begin to think seriously to ourselves, "Is there something more

I can do about this?"

Indeed, there are specific positive measures that can be taken to gain some control over the way suggestions influence us. The first step in this process is to assume an attitude of self-observation with respect to each and every suggestion. Notice how suggestions influence your mental and physical state. You might observe, for example, how you feel when you are reading a newspaper article about a bombing. You may begin to notice how your muscles tense up as your favorite football team misses a field goal in the closing moments of the game and loses, how your body becomes rigid as you watch a murder being committed in a TV drama.

As your observations go on and your sensitivity increases, you will become aware that each event carries with it suggestions which continue to influence you long after the event has passed. Even in those cases when you are not directly told to buy a certain product or perform a certain action, still each experience that you have creates an attitude or set of beliefs in your mind, leading you in a particular direction and into a particular set of further experiences. Thus the tension over the lost football game may leave the unconscious suggestion of disappointment and frustration which is later expressed when you relate to your family or friends.

Each experience that we have has a lasting effect upon us. For example, a student told us how he was watching a television show before sitting down to meditate. Ordinarily he wouldn't notice the effect of the earlier experience, because he would immediately become engaged in another activity which would distract his

mind. But when he sat down to meditate after watching
the show, trying to quiet his mind and bring it to a calm
center, he became aware of all the subtle thoughts
connected with the show he had just seen. The drama that
he had just witnessed was still vivid. He was unable to
calm his mind. Instead of being able to concentrate on
the object of meditation, he felt pulled here and there by
his recall of the conflicts and actions of the drama.

In this way each and every experience we have leaves
its residue. Every thought, every action, every word that
we have ever spoken leaves an imprint on our unconscious
mind and influences those experiences we will have in the
future. Perhaps you have noticed that if you listen to a
song just before going to bed at night, you may wake up
the next morning whistling the tune. You may puzzle
over why that tune is sticking in your mind until you
later recall that you had heard it the night before.

Each experience we have is exactly like a wave made
by a boat. As a motorboat travels along on a lake the
waves spread out, growing smaller as their distance from
the boat increases, yet remaining long after the boat
has gone by. Similarly the full impact of an event is
experienced at the moment it occurs. But a wave spreads
out from the center of that experience. The amplitude
of the wave gradually diminishes but the effect remains
nevertheless. A day, ten days or a month later it is still
with us. Often you are not aware of the lingering waves
of each experience because, in the meantime, many other
experiences have come by and created their own waves.
The disturbed action on the surface of your mind created
by these new events seems to cancel out the action of the

earlier waves but this is not so. They are merely hidden by the bigger and more recent waves in the turbulence of your mental functions. It is only through freeing your mind from new disruptions that you will become aware of the remaining subtle effects of earlier waves. The waves from previous experiences will then be seen as creating a continued disturbance in the calmness of the mind.

The Conflicting Nature of Suggestions

The confusion and contradictory nature of the many suggestions which come to us in our everyday life reflect the confusion and uncertainty in the culture from which they spring. Many people are uncertain about the purpose and meaning of life. They are unsure of what to do with the time they have at their disposal. In their confusion they turn toward others to find answers about who they are, why they exist, and how their life should be lived. Often they look toward leaders, not realizing that those in authoritative positions may not have answered such questions for themselves and are, perhaps, looking for solutions to the same problems. So the answers come back scattered and unfulfilling.

Those around us follow now one fad and then another in the search for meaning and purpose. Yesterday they suggested that we try psychoanalysis as a way of finding who we are, then encounter groups or LSD, then women's liberation, "swinging," transactional analysis, and primal scream therapy were in turn suggested as avenues to explore in finding ourselves. Each person looks toward another for an answer. And others pass on what they heard the day before, although unsure of it themselves. All of the many suggestions that confound us are attempts to find meaningful answers to who and what we are. But most are confused, partial answers which come from mirages that on closer examination do not contain the fulfillment which we seek.

Most of us have spent a great part of our life in looking here and there for who we are. Even when we have established a seemingly solid outer identity, deep within us there is a basic uncertainty and lack of solidity. Although we may identify with our job and family, we seek out other relationships that may add further meaning to our lives. Each and every one of us has found ourselves walking down long dark streets in the night, hoping to find someone who would provide that ultimate answer. Perhaps we have looked toward a person of the opposite sex, toward an ideology, an organization, or our own power which would lead other people to tell us that we are right. But most of the time whatever we have found proves to be disillusioning in the end, and we must take up the search anew. We try one experience after the other, read books, scan the media, and cultivate new relationships in an attempt to find a definition of ourselves. We are all like the infant who comes into the world with large uncertain eyes, looking here and there, trying to understand it. Although we pretend as if we do, as if it all makes sense, beneath the surface exterior that we show to others the infant remains looking even now.

We keep hoping to find someone special to lead us and show us the way to abiding happiness, joy and peace.

We look first toward our parents but, as we grow, we become disappointed in them, realizing that they after all did not really know and understand. Then, as we grow further, we idealize a man or a woman and may even marry them, thinking that they will provide meaning and fulfillment in our life. Later when we become disenchanted, we may seek to have children as a way of overcoming our uncertainty. But parents, wife, husband, children or friends, cannot fulfill the role of the Knower that we would have them play. They are not the perfect one we seek. So we often leave our relationships disappointed, and then perhaps seek someone else. But ordinary mortals cannot provide the answer for us, and it is unfair and unreasonable to ask them to solve our problems and endow our lives with meaning. As long as we look toward others, toward objects or experiences in the world to provide answers to life's riddles, we will go on experiencing confusion, for it is a situation in which the blind are leading the blind.

Seeing the hopelessness of finding answers from other people who are themselves in a state of confusion, we might begin to question the many suggestions which come toward us creating perplexity in our own minds. We might begin at this point to ask ourselves, "Is there any value in letting myself be influenced by the confusing suggestions that come my way? Are there some suggestions which are more helpful to me than others? Are there some which would help me to be more centered, more peaceful and more joyful, rather than lead me toward confusion, anxiety and scattered attention? Is it possible for me to determine what suggestions I will encounter and how much effect they will have on me?"

Suggestion and Hypnosis

> In the beginning, I was one person, knowing nothing but
> my own experience. Then I was told things, and I became
> two people. . . .
> In the beginning was I, and I was good.
> Then came in other I. Outside authority. This was confusing.
> And then other I became *very* confused because there were so
> many different outside authorities.
> Sit nicely. Leave the room to blow your nose. Don't do
> that, that's silly. . . . Flush the toilet at night because if you
> don't it makes it harder to clean. DON'T FLUSH THE
> TOILET AT NIGHT—you wake people up! Always be nice to
> people. Even if you don't like them, you mustn't hurt their
> feelings. Be frank and honest. If you don't tell people what
> you think of them, that's cowardly. . . .
> The most important thing is to have a career. The most
> important thing is to get married. The hell with everyone.
> Be nice to everyone. The most important thing is sex. The
> most important thing is to have money in the bank. The most
> important thing is to have everyone like you. . . . The most
> important thing is to be sophisticated and say what you don't
> mean and don't let anyone know what you feel. The most
> important thing is to be ahead of everyone else. The most
> important thing is a black seal coat and china and silver. . . .
> The most important thing is to love your parents. . . . The
> most important thing is to be independent. . . . The most
> important thing is to be dutiful to your husband. . . . The
> most important thing is to go to the right plays and read the
> right books. The most important thing is to do what others
> say. And others say all these things. . . .
> Out of all the other I's some are chosen as a pattern that is
> me . . . and sometimes these take over. Then who am I?*

---

* Carl R. Rogers and Barry Stevens, *Person to Person,* Real People Press,
Lafayette, California, 1967, p. 1-2.

We have focused until now primarily on the suggestions that come to us in our everyday living as adults. But it is important to realize that suggestions have played an important role from the earliest stages of our childhood. It is largely the suggestions given to us as young children, especially by our parents, that have helped to shape the self-concept which we have as adults. R. D. Laing, the British psychiatrist, has expressed the idea that we have actually become hypnotized through our childhood family experiences into believing that we are a particular type of person. He says, "I consider that the majority of adults (including myself) are or have been, more or less, in a post-hypnotic trance, induced in early infancy."*

Perhaps as you were growing up, your parents would say to you again and again, "You're naughty," or "You're bad," or "You're smart," or "You're lazy." They attributed to you particular qualities and to these your teachers, friends, and classmates added further attributions. Gradually these became reinforced and established as a part of your self-definition. The particular qualities that were emphasized for you became the keystone of your personality. So now you think of yourself as being a person who is lazy, or bad or whatever. You think you are the particular character that has been molded by these suggestions.

In this way we are all hypnotized into believing that we are a particular kind of person. All the other

* R. D. Laing, *The Politics of the Family*, CBC Publications, Toronto, 1969, p. 14.

possibilities of what we may be, are excluded from our firmly established self-concept. Even if our way of defining ourselves and acting is non-productive, even if it leads to severe emotional and psychological turmoil, we are often unable to let go of those attributions which we have come to believe are part and parcel of our very nature. But if we are to grow we must awaken from our hypnotic trance. This process of awakening is depicted in the following story:

> A pride of lions which included a pregnant lioness was attacking a flock of sheep. In the midst of this, some hunters appeared on the scene and began shooting. During the confusion, the lioness gave birth to a cub, but in fleeing from the hunters, she was forced to abandon it. The cub followed the sheep as they too ran off. Since it was helpless and unable to take care of itself, the sheep fostered it. After living amongst them for some time, the young lion began to identify himself with them. He learned to become easily frightened, to feel weak and defenseless. Instead of roaring like a lion, he began to bleat like the other sheep around him.
>
> One day the sheep were again attacked by some lions. The cub was terrified and started running away. But one of the lions noticed him amidst the sheep. He overtook him and asked him what he was doing there. Then he realized that the cub thought he was a lamb. No matter what he said he was unable to convince the cub that he really was a lion. Finally he took him to the edge of a clear lake and told him to look at his reflection. With this direct experience the cub was astonished to realize that he was not, after all, what he had imagined himself to be.

So it is with each of us. We have formed concepts of ourselves which are not accurate. They are based on the limitations set by others or on suggestions that come from external sources. The therapist, the spiritual guide, the guru, or any other person who is a true teacher, leads us to look at the mirror image of ourselves. He leads us beyond suggestions to see things more clearly as they are. Such a teacher comes along and says, "Wake up! That's not really who you are. These qualities that you have used to define yourself are merely superficial. There is much, much more in you, a deeper essence that is very different from your own notions. You're not really lazy, or selfish, or whatever you thought you were. Deep within you there is a fountain of joy, love and wisdom which is your real nature. See for yourself. These are your real qualities, rather than the more superficial characteristics that you have been hypnotized into accepting." In this way each of us is called to awaken from our hypnotic sleep, to become de-hypnotized, and to experience new possibilities of who and what we may be.

In the initial stages of yogic training, the student learns to replace negative suggestions with positive ones. Finally he is led to that direct experience which is beyond any influence of suggestion. While most of the suggestions to which we are exposed in everyday living are random and scattered, the suggestions given in yogic teaching are aimed at leading the student again and again toward direct experience. Instead of contradicting one another, they are all pointed in the same direction. Through these suggestions, the aspirant is guided toward letting go of his previously built-up fears, anxieties, worries and self-concept. He is led time and again to focus his attention on the present moment, to be aware of his bodily sensations, breathing, or thoughts as he experiences them. He learns to develop an observing attitude instead of being caught up in the extraneous suggestions that continually appear before the mind. Since suggestion is one of the chief ways in which we learn, we can redirect the process so that the suggestions we choose to follow are those which lead us toward our goal. But we have to go beyond the suggestive process. Yoga teaches us how to gain mastery over suggestions and to experience for ourselves.

The Process of De-hypnotization

The person who has no clear purpose or center in his life is easily swayed by suggestions. All suggestions may seem equally valid and worth following. As a result of this he is easily tossed here and there. He has no real basis for evaluating the suggestions that come before him. But as soon as one establishes a purpose, each suggestion can be appraised in terms of fulfilling it. For example, if you wish to learn to play the piano, and this is an important goal for you, then you can choose to follow those suggestions which will improve your skill and to ignore those which may be detrimental. If you have a routine practice time and if someone suggests that you go out with him to a show, your sense of purpose and determination will lead you to pass that temptation by. Thus it is with each of the goals we establish for ourselves. They provide specific centers of organization for us and allow us to exert some control over the various suggestions with which we are confronted. Unfortunately, many of the goals that we choose are quite temporary and often based on poorly considered suggestions, unrealistic fantasies, or erroneous self-concepts. Thus learning to play the piano may guide your actions and eliminate the influence of alien suggestions for a certain period of time; but then you may realize that you have no great talent, become disillusioned with that goal, and turn to a new center of organization.

The stronger and more lasting is one's commitment to a purpose, the greater one's control over suggestions will be. However, many of us do not have enduring commitments. There is no clear sense of any inherent purpose which life itself gives to us, so we flit about seeking one pleasure or goal and then another. We take up an attractive new project for a time, but after a while become tired of it, give it up and find a new belief, a new cause, a new center around which we can temporarily establish a part of our identity. Perhaps we may find a spiritual teacher or group and throw our energy into following them "wholeheartedly" for a while. But then our interest wanes; we become disillusioned and seek another purpose. Sooner or later we will find that most of the purposes and goals which we establish for ourselves are temporary and illusory.

But those who have expanded their consciousness and experienced that higher knowledge have found that there is an underlying purpose to our lives which remains stable despite all the changes that we undergo. We have seen that there is an evolutionary process of growth, that we develop along a path of gaining greater and greater consciousness. If we could see our lives objectively we would recognize this pattern of growth and align our conscious goals with it. However, all too often, we ignore this underlying purpose and instead engage in pursuits based on more superficial and transitory desires and on the various suggestions that come our way. As a result, we experience disunity, chaos and confusion.

We are all on a journey. Our destination is a state in which our consciousness is expanded to that limit at which our identity is not narrowly confined but embraces all. This is the underlying goal that each of us has, the ultimate purpose of our existence. Whether we are consciously aware of it or not, we are all traveling in this direction. Through the many experiences we have, we are moving closer and closer toward that final destination.

Our journey would be fast and direct if we were to stay on the main path, to keep our aim within our conscious awareness and choose only those experiences and suggestions which keep us centered in that development. But we encounter many allurements which lead us from the most direct path. We leave the way to fulfill countless desires. We seek experiences which promise happiness, but sooner or later we come to find that these side trips are filled with seductive promises that remain unfulfilled. They contain only those pleasures that are mixed with grief and unpleasant emotions. Each time we wander from the main course we become involved in a real-life drama. A whole world is created in which certain desires may be fulfilled, but in the course of which we also suffer. We return again and again to the path, giving up those charms and temptations which we have examined and which in the end we found incomplete.

The wants and desires which we have may take us off the main path only for a short time, or we may become entangled in a side trip for a lifetime. But the many experiences that we have aid in the expansion of awareness, ultimately helping us to progress on our journey. Those side trips which lead us toward more narrowly conceived pleasures or goals enable us to fulfill desires which are latent within us. They provide us with the opportunity of attaining a coveted goal and becoming aware of its limitations. Through the pain and misery that we find associated with fantasized pleasure, we come to realize its insufficiency and turn back toward the path.

Such a journey can become long and tortuous. But it is actually not necessary to take up each of the tempting suggestions and to intensify the desire for that experience within us to a point where we feel compelled to fulfill it. It is possible for us to learn to lay aside those suggestions which will not help us in the most direct progress on our journey. We can avoid coming into contact with suggestions that will lead us on many side tracks, and we can learn how to minimize the effect of other suggestions that would also delay our progress.

It may be helpful for you to evaluate the suggestions which come before you each day. Which of these lead you toward greater awareness of your ultimate purpose in life, and which lead you toward distraction and slow down your progress? When you listen to the radio or watch television, when you meet and talk with your friends, does the information coming to you direct your mind again and again to the path of your development or does it pull you away? Do the suggestions coming before you make you more restless and confused or do they help you center yourself? Once you have uncovered those suggestions which are disturbing and distracting, you can begin to work on eliminating their influence.

Many of us feel obligated to remain in contact with the suggestions which are upsetting to us. We think that if we do not worry about the disturbing news of the world, if we do not keep up with what is going on, we will be left out and, furthermore, we will not be able to help in correcting things. However, when our own mind is made restless, we are not very able to set things aright. It is only when we have balanced our mind and become steadfastly aware of the basic purpose in life that we can confront unpleasant suggestions without being overpowered by them. Only then will we be able to have a corrective influence on the disturbance around us.

A great many of the suggestions which upset us are not so intense. They come rather from the entertainment and diversion which we seek, but which carries with it its own frustration. There are many disturbing suggestions in your everyday living that could be avoided with a little bit of thought. If the activities caused by these suggestions were left out of your life, your sense of peace and tranquility would be greatly increased.

A great sage of the last century, Ramakrishna, told his students that when they first become aware of the path of self-development, they should isolate themselves from negative suggestions. He compared them to a young tree. A tree that has just sprung from the earth is easily overwhelmed by the environment in which it finds itself.

If the tree is growing on your lawn, it might quickly be cut down along with the grass, or in a field its leaves might be eaten by a grazing cow. If we wish a young tree to grow, we often put a fence around it for protection. The tree matures and becomes strong and, after some time, it no longer needs that protective fence. The lawn mower or the grazing cattle can no longer harm it.

Thus, as we grow we are more able to live in the midst of contrary and disturbing suggestions without being so easily influenced by them. As we become centered in our purpose, as we remain conscious of the larger journey we are on, we become capable of facing suggestions which lead us toward other goals without being swayed by them. We then are able to live in the chaos and confusion of the world yet remain calm and serene. At this point we become a source of inspiration and guidance to others, and our journey toward our ultimate goal is more swift and sure. For we are centered on the *summum bonum* (supreme goal) toward which we are headed.

Suggestions We Give Ourselves

We have thus far talked about the way we are influenced by suggestions through the media, from our parents when we were still young, and from the friends and acquaintances with whom we spend our time. But there is a fourth source of suggestive influence—our own selves. We often give ourselves suggestions about who and what we are, in the form of thoughts or subliminal attitudes, for example, such ideas as "I'll fail again; I'm not very good; I'll never get anywhere with this."

Originally such negative suggestions may have come from others, but at some point we accepted them as part of ourselves and began shaping our lives around our belief in them. Many of us indulge in negative thoughts of all sorts—depressive thoughts, thoughts of failure, fears. These suggestions have become habitual for us. We have learned to live with them, thinking that this is the way we are. But we can learn to handle such suggestions just the same way as those suggestions which come from the outside world. We must first learn to observe them occurring without identifying with them. Then we can consciously and systematically replace them with more helpful and positive suggestions which serve a better purpose, leading us to expanded consciousness. It is helpful, for example, to work with positive ideas and phrases, repeating them again and again. As they become part of us a new self-concept is created.

Perhaps the way you have allowed yourself to be influenced by suggestions until now has led you to feel that you are not confident or capable. If you are a teacher and go to a class feeling unsure of yourself, afraid that the students may not like you, that you may have nothing to say, this suggestion will become a reality. You will project your negative attitude and lack of enthusiasm, and the class will begin to receive your message. But with a little thought it would be easy to create constructive suggestions and, as a result, a completely different environment. Simply by taking a few minutes and focusing on positive thoughts you can completely alter your own attitude and that of others toward you. You can easily develop the kind of attitude you want. If you use suggestion to create a feeling of confidence, your teaching will be enhanced. Your suggestions will create the experience of success.

Many of us allow ourselves to be overwhelmed by the events of the day. If things don't go well, if we've had a bad day, we may feel like a failure. If we have an accident with our car, if we lose our wallet, forget an appointment or act clumsily, we become upset with ourselves, feeling that perhaps we should have stayed in bed. We may feel all of the events of the day piling up and resulting in the attitude: "I just can't do anything right." This, for the moment, becomes our self-concept. It may become a part of our permanent identity if we allow that attitude to stay with us, for it will continue to create more experiences of failure. But if you can become conscious of how these internal suggestions are shaping your experienced world, you can then begin to take control over them. This is a simple process. It merely takes consistently paying attention to your state of mind and introducing constructive suggestions to change the whole complexion of your outlook.

We must teach ourselves not to take so seriously that transitory self-concept which we have built up through the day. We can learn to disengage ourselves from it and to establish a new way of defining ourselves. The suggestions that we give ourselves mold our perception of the world. We tend to think that there is one absolute reality out there, and that it appears the same to all. But actually each person experiences the world differently from the next. To some the world is harsh and cruel, people seem cynical and ready to take advantage of them. Others may face the same world with a feeling of joy and trust, believing that those they meet are ready to give what they can. There is not any one reality. The negative, harsh reality created by one person is just as subjective as the positive reality created by another. The trouble is that all too often we allow the suggestions of other people to affect our notions about ourselves. We incorporate these suggestions and in turn create an image of the world in which we live. But it is also possible to substitute our own selected suggestions in place of those which have been programmed in by others, and use these positive suggestions to create a more positive world.

Direct Experience

In addition to describing negative and positive suggestion, we want to go further and explain more about the source of direct knowledge. Direct experience with the help of sense perception is not that knowledge of which we are talking. We are explaining that knowledge which helps in seeing the whole and not a part of the thing observed. Seeing the horizon through a narrow window is different from seeing the horizon from the roof. Direct knowledge reveals all the inner and outer secrets. Sense perception is superficial and thus cannot be considered higher knowledge. When we hear about something we doubt, but when we receive direct knowledge there is no doubt at all. All the doubts are removed and replaced by a tranquility which is very necessary for receiving the higher and direct experience from the deeper levels of our being.

The source of direct knowledge is within us. It is part of an infinite library of knowledge within. Both the negative and positive suggestions which come from without, fall into the category of indirect knowledge. They cannot be considered the means of attaining higher knowledge. Direct knowledge is received from the center of consciousness through systematic practices and disciplines. The *Upanishads* say that when the mind is purified, made one-pointed and led to the center of consciousness, then higher knowledge is available. The wise ones and sages received this knowledge in all times and climes and in all cultures.

Raja Yoga explains how this is achieved in four steps. First the mind is not allowed to be dissipated in the external world by the avenues called senses. Then the mind is to be concentrated on the object of meditation. When the mind and object of meditation become one, concentration starts flowing uninterruptedly. Finally one establishes direct contact with the source of higher knowledge. Before reaching this state, one must learn to free his mind from his own thinking process, emotional disorders and subtle desires of the mundane world. This method is not taught in the world, but those fortunate few who have followed it were able to go to the center of consciousness and get freedom from all miseries, pains and ignorance.

The Vedantic way of receiving this knowledge is to sit near a competent and realized teacher and listen to the scriptures which are revelations of the great sages. Then the aspirant contemplates and attains a state of clarity. He learns to distinguish that experience which is unalloyed from those which are mingled with the indirect knowledge called suggestions. The final state which is called perfection, void, *samadhi* and *sakshatkara* is possible by following this path of Jnana Yoga.

When a student starts following this path with full determination and goes through all the preliminaries taught by the teacher, he clearly differentiates between these two varieties of knowledge, the direct and indirect. Such a student, though he might find a few difficulties in following this rare path, finally attains a state of peace, wisdom and happiness. Such a man lives in the world as an example and serves humanity.

The learning process today makes one an outsider while this other process makes one an insider. Fortunate are those who know that all things happen inside first, before they are reflected outside. The world of direct experience offers satisfaction and complete knowledge, whereas the world outside offers a knowledge which definitely needs the process of filtration. When mind becomes one-pointed and sharp enough to understand the quality of knowledge gained from within and the quantity received from outside, then it understands the value of unalloyed knowledge not based on suggestion, but on direct experience.

4

The Play and Drama of Life

> The visible universe is nothing else than a theater representative of the Lord's kingdom, and this latter is a theater representative of the Lord himself.
>
> Emanuel Swedenborg

The theme of the above quotation is also found in the *Bhagavatam* in which Krishna says, "This theater, the world, is meant for my *lila* (joy). One who understands this lives peacefully in union with me."

Life is exactly like a drama full of tragedy, comedy, mystery and adventure; from childhood until his last breath, a human being goes on playing his role, consciously and unconsciously, in this drama of life. When the child is born he finds a circumscribed theater around him called family. He is amazed at watching the games played with him and around him—everyone seems to love him. When he starts playing with other children, building castles in the sand he is very pleased with these dramas. For quite some time his toys are very real and he hugs his teddy bear as a grownup hugs another living being. But after some time this is no longer a reality for him and he leaves these toys behind. He starts entering the real drama of life when he begins communicating with other children. He appreciates or sometimes feels dejected when his skills are challenged by others. During his childhood he thinks that this is reality, but when his consciousness grows further he becomes aware of several other plays and games of life. He goes on playing dramas his whole life but at last comes to know that all of these dramas and games have not satisfied him. Finally he thinks of playing a drama with the Lord. He starts brooding on what this play is all about. He asks himself, "Why have I come here?" This is the final drama for a human being.

There are various levels of drama, which unfold as awareness expands. We might wonder, is there anything beyond dramas, is there any reality? Yes, there is. He who has manifest to become all of this is beyond the dramas of life. The *Upanishads* say, "There is only one unity in all of this diversity."

Play Versus Reality

We typically divide our world into two different kinds of experience which we call "play" and "reality." Each appears to have different qualities. Play seems to be somewhat insubstantial, transitory and not to be taken too seriously. Reality, on the other hand, is usually considered to be quite serious, permanent and solid. But if we take a closer look we shall realize that the differences between these two realms are not always clear.

Consider staged plays as an example. What is their purpose—to provide us with entertainment but, more importantly, to help us understand or cope with some aspect of our lives. We dress up, pretend to be someone else, and act out a role in order more fully to experience, objectify and gain consciousness of our feelings, attitudes, thoughts and unconscious processes. And sometimes we may even become so absorbed in the acting that we forget it is a play and take it for real.

The plays which we create are extremely valuable. By watching a drama presented on the stage, we learn how others handle situations similar to those we face in life. We can experiment, through the actors, with different possibilities for dealing with these situations. We also learn how to establish for ourselves the perspective of being outside the drama. Though we may identify to some extent with the actors, crying or gripping the seat in terror during the more intense moments of the plot, for the most part we keep our sense of witness to the whole show. Whether we are watching a TV melodrama or a play by Shakespeare, we maintain a more or less objective attitude toward our unconscious hopes and fears, brought to the surface by the unfolding spectacle. Watching the story of a doctor operating on his patient or of a criminal being prosecuted by the police helps us to live out our fantasies without becoming involved "body and soul" in similar real-life situations. Thus we learn to act out our desires and to cope with a variety of situations in the least painful way possible.

This use of play has even been extended into more formal psychotherapy where "psychodrama" is used to allow group participants to act out conflict and gain some perspective on it. By acting out their personal drama in the therapy session, they learn how to observe themselves objectively. They can also learn how to avoid acting out their drama in real life with their families or friends—situations in which they are more likely to become caught up in the tensions and harmful emotions that the drama engenders.

The word "play" has, of course, another important meaning. It is used not only for those formalized dramas that are shown on the stage but also for those that are created by children in their everyday living. In their play children often experiment with various roles that they might assume later in adulthood. They play at being mother or father, at having a home of their own. They make up plays in which they pretend to be working in different professions such as doctor or school teacher.

But as we grow older, this role-playing is continued on a more serious level. When we adopt such roles as student, high school athlete, boyfriend or girlfriend, when we emerge into adulthood, and settle down to the routine of work, acquiring the necessities and luxuries of life, establishing a niche in the community, we take all of these activities to be ever so important. As we grow, our experimenting with various roles seems to be more serious and to be more related to what we call "reality."

When we form a habit of playing various roles we reach a point where we have identified with the world and with the situations in which we find ourselves. Many of us feel this suffocating sickness in our daily life when the world seems to annihilate our whole existence. This happens when we lose our consciousness of reality and give increasing attention to the drama of life.

This tendency to take play seriously can exist regardless of age. Even if involved in a game, children are likely to become so absorbed in their play that they forget the make-believe. For instance, in a game of chess winning becomes all-important and if the child loses he gets very upset. He begins to act jealous or hostile toward his opponent. All sorts of undesirable and unpleasant emotions may arise if play becomes too important and the goal overrides the immediate enjoyment of the process.

This is exactly the same situation in which many adults find themselves. They become emotional and disturbed if the cards of "real life" do not go their way. They forget that they are merely playing a part and become absorbed in and identified with the role of the moment. They become caught up in the apparent stakes of the game, feeling that it is a life-and-death situation, that all their happiness or unhappiness depends on the outcome of the scene being played.

Involvement Versus Renunciation

There are some characters who are considered successful in playing their roles while others are considered unsuccessful. The whole secret of playing one's role is in knowing the technique of playing it and yet living above the role. Suppose all the characters of the drama in a particular theater start playing each other's role. Can you imagine what will be the fate of that theater and what that drama will be called? There is some value in playing this drama of life with the sense that the drama is real up to a certain extent, because if one does not know how to play one's own role he might disturb the whole drama of life and might disturb himself as well. So often we play the roles without being trained and thus conflict is created between our inner and external behavior. This conflict becomes the cause of constant problems within, and might even sow the seeds of many psychosomatic diseases.

There is a problem in playing the role either way. If one plays one's role with unified mind and actions even then one loses awareness of the reality and is swayed by the charms and temptations of the drama; and if he performs his actions just to play the drama, but does not put his mind and heart in it, he cannot play his role well. This conflict has created a great problem, for intellectuals especially, in understanding how to play one's role skillfully and not be lost in this drama.

In all times and places there have been wise people who have dived deep into the problems and conflicts of life. Three opinions have been put forth about how to relate to the world. Some say renounce all this and seek truth; the *Isha Upanishad* offers the alternative of becoming absorbed in the drama of life for a hundred years. But both of these extremes seem to be impractical. Others have found the solution to this dilemma in perfecting the art of living and being. They say that to escape from this theater is cowardice, but to live in the world and remain above is the main purpose of an actor. This can be perfected by constant vigilance over the actions, feelings and thoughts.

This third group of wise men says that no matter where you live you cannot live without playing your role. You should develop three qualities in your character by asking: (1) Can I play my role in a way so that it does not become an obstacle? (2) Can it become a means? (3) Can I go on playing my role, maintaining my awareness of the Reality? Janaka, Socrates, and Ramakrishna are the rare examples of those who follow this tradition.

The *Bhagavad Gita* also takes this point of view, saying that one who has known the technique of performing his duties skillfully and selflessly, easily crosses the mire of delusion. In the drama of the *Bhagavad Gita*, Arjuna, the spiritual aspirant, is taking part in a civil war. His role is to lead one side against the other. But he does not want to fight and kill. He is so identified with his opponents that he sinks down in despair. The first thing that Arjuna is taught in this situation is to see his current role in a larger perspective so that he can understand that the way in which he is participating is really only one scene in a whole series of dramas. Krishna, his spiritual guide, suggests that he need not take it so seriously, for all of these actors, even if they are killed in their performance, will soon be given a new body and a new role in a play still to come.* Though they may lose their parts in this drama they will eventually be given many others in numerous other dramas still to be performed. The Grand Drama will continue on with the same cast, now portraying one character, now another.

---

*That this understanding does not give one license to act irresponsibly will be seen in chapter six, entitled "Freedom and Responsibility."

These statements of the *Bhagavad Gita* make it clear that we need not identify with one particular portrayal. This entire life is merely a drama within a drama within a drama. The performance today is just one of innumerable scenes, perhaps scene number 23,711 in the million scenes of one lifetime. And according to Upanishadic psychology, this is only one lifetime out of thousands. If you can imagine that your being is a huge, intricate and beautiful tapestry, then you might think of one lifetime as just one tiny stitch in the grand design. Do not take it as seriously as if it were the whole show. Do not become emotionally caught up in this single stitch, so says the *Bhagavad Gita.*

This understanding can help us in extricating ourselves from the frustrations and conflicts which we have. It can help us loosen our attachment to the character we have taken in this particular lifetime. You need no longer believe that you really are the character that you are playing on this stage of life. You can wake up to realize that you are different from the role you are playing. The being who you really are is different from the costume of this body. You are different from your outer form. You are not the person whom you have up to now defined yourself to be.

We are involved simultaneously in a number of scenes and plots within this grand play of life which goes on around and about us. Most of the plots are far from original; they can be found on stage or screen, in songs, novels, myths and fairytales. They have recognized names such as "Revenge," "Jealousy," "Outlaw," "Save me, save me," or "I am the boss." We shift from one plot to another within our own limited repertoire as the occasion requires. In the course of each day, with each of our co-actors, we are called upon to take different attitudes and to engage in different relationships and roles. All of our unhappiness and suffering in life comes from taking our part in the drama to be too solid and too absolute. But alas, one becomes aware of this reality very late in life. One of the Persian poets says "when I had strength I did not have wisdom, now I have wisdom but not strength." Finally we all become aware of the hollowness of our roles. But if by chance someone awakens from the sleep of ignorance he understands that roles should be played, yet awareness of the reality should not be lost. The *Gita* says meditation in action is the key for success; wherever you go remain aware of the center within you.

Few understand this wisdom. Many people have become dissatisfied and unhappy with the parts that they have been given to play in this great drama. Perhaps you have the part of a parent who must take care of a young child, or the part of a son or daughter who must provide for elderly parents but find such a task too demanding or too difficult to cope with. Most of us, at one time or another, have had roles which we would like to avoid or cast off. Rather than acting out our part we would like to "leave the scene."

It is typically human to think that we can escape from undesirable roles by changing the scenery or the cast of characters with whom we are relating, in the hope of creating a new scene with greater potential for happiness. In counseling, we have encountered many individuals who desperately seek to alter the circumstances of their unhappy personal dramas. Some, for example, have gotten divorced. More often than not, they soon become involved again in a similar predicament with their next boyfriend or girlfriend, husband or wife, and the show goes on with a new character playing the opposite part. Some people try to bring about a magical transformation in their lives by moving from one place to another. When conflict or turmoil is experienced, they think that by going to a new city or getting a new job they will alter the drama, leaving the problems behind with the old props. They are convinced that being in a new situation will prevent further trouble, only to discover after a while that this does not work.

Several years ago one of the authors was a counselor at a Midwestern university. Many of the students who came for help had grown up in New York and had chosen to go to school in the Midwest. They felt that they could get away from family conflicts by putting a thousand miles of distance between themselves and their parents. They also thought that they could escape from the harshness and callousness of big city life by going to school in a small town where people might be more open and friendly. Typically, these young men and women continued to experience emotional turmoil, for they had brought their family conflicts along with them as a part of their mental baggage. Although they were physically distant, their thoughts kept returning to scenes with their parents and others back home. Because of their attitudes and habits they also found it difficult to form new friendships with the less sophisticated Midwesterners.

They sought out others who had come from New York and who were having similar difficulties. So in their attempt to run away from an unpleasant life they had actually recreated their old life style in a new setting.

Other individuals who are involved in a drama of spiritual unfoldment may seek to avoid the unpleasantness of their life situations by becoming "renunciates." They may fantasize themselves going off to India and spending their time alone in a cave, sitting in meditation for hour after hour. But if they were to act out this desire they would find that in the stillness of that cave their imagination would be busily recreating the dramas and the scenes from the past. The mind would also be restless with the desire to participate in new plays, and this withdrawal from the habitual life style would quickly become unbearable.

The trouble is that when we leave the old scene and create a new one we find ourselves wishing to return to where we were. Being in one drama we want to experience another, and when we have created another we long for the first. We oscillate back and forth, discontented with the show going on at the present moment and unable to disengage ourselves from the desire for something else.

Perhaps you do not go to the extent of travelling to India but sit down quietly at home to meditate, temporarily withdrawing from your involvement in outward activities to find a center of rest within yourself. But even here you discover that your mind is not satisfied to be where it is. Parts of the drama you have been playing draw your attention away from the peace of meditation. You worry about your job, your relations with others, or about your future. Thus many dramas are created and come before your mind's eye in the course of your attempt to meditate.

If all these thoughts and fantasies were to be acted out, they would take on the solidity of "real life" experiences. In the beginning stages of meditation we learn how to keep these potential dramas at the level of thoughts rather than have them actualized and be overwhelmed by them. In more advanced stages, the meditator realizes that thoughts are in themselves dramas which have a solidity of their own and keep the mind in a state of turmoil. He understands how all of the predicaments which he calls real grow from the seeds of desire in his mind, and he learns how to center his mind so that even these seeds cannot grow.

The first step in solving our problems is to understand that nothing is accomplished by running away from our drama, for it occurs all the time in our own minds. When we come to this realization, we know that there is no short and easy way to eliminate or alter undesirable situations. The path of dropping out, changing the scene or renouncing certain modes of life turns out not to be fruitful. Since we are the creators of our own drama, we can get out of it not by transposing the play but only by transforming ourselves, so that we can begin to create something entirely new.

We must realize that the way to change outward circumstances is not to leave them but to turn inward and work on the very source of the anxieties and conflicts that we are experiencing. From this point of view it does not matter whether we find ourselves in one type of situation or another. The internal drama may be the same regardless of external events, and we must focus our energy on bringing about a change from within.

A man who had just died was given the choice of going to heaven with a hateful and deceitful man as a companion, or going to hell along with a saint. He immediately chose to go to hell, saying, "The first man will make a hell out of heaven, but the saint will make a heaven from hell."

Whether one is in isolation or amidst a multitude of worldly activities, the opportunity to grow and develop presents itself in every situation. It is not necessary to escape from what you may consider a personal predicament in order to have the proper atmosphere for growth. The really crucial thing is how you deal with the situation in which you find yourself and how you deal with the situations that are going on inside your head. You can make out of your circumstances a big melodrama with all kinds of negative emotions: fears, disappointments and anxieties. Or you can learn to avoid feeling entrapped in the play in which you are cast. Whether you find happiness and joy in life depends on what attitude you assume toward your role in this grand drama. If you could see in each of your experiences the potential for learning, you could use every situation in a constructive way.

If you were an artist and wanted to paint a picture, you could not do so unless you first found some material with which to work. You would have to collect some canvas, a frame, some paints and brushes and other accessories. Without these, though you had the perfect idea for a painting and all the skill required to create what you envision, you could do nothing. Our circumstances are the materials we need in order to create ourselves, in order to develop the hidden potential within us. The world with all its dramas and the particular drama in which we find ourselves exist in order to provide the material for our growth and development. Without this drama of life the growth of consciousness could not occur. The circumstances in which we find ourselves provide the very lessons we need in order to expand our awareness. When our consciousness is more limited we become caught up in the insecurity of the ever-changing flow. We seek to cling to that which is pleasurable and to avoid what is difficult or painful. But when we gain greater perspective we see beyond the immediate pleasures and pains to the larger purpose of the show which is unfolding in our midst. We see that all this has been created so that we can learn the lessons of life and finally understand who and what we really are.

The Process of Growth

The way in which we grow psychologically and spiritually is through the process of disidentifying with the roles we have been playing, and with the person we thought we were. There are two basic ways of learning to disidentify with our roles. The more painful way is through enacting many unpleasant scenes until the suffering outweighs our anticipated pleasure and we change our part. Imagine that a married man is having an affair with a woman. He plays the part of a clandestine lover. He is caught up in the drama of that situation with its enjoyments and its miseries. He worries: "When can I get away to see her again? Will my wife find out? If I leave my wife, what will become of the children?" As the drama unfolds, the concerns, remorse and conflicts may begin to outweigh the pleasure and eventually may even overcome his desire to be with her. Then the protagonist may decide that he does not wish to go on. By going through the situation he learns that becoming involved in this way is not worth the pain it engenders.

This is the slow and unconscious way of learning. We become aware of the consequences after we receive the unhappy results of our actions. The conscious way is to see the consequences ahead of time using the knowledge we have gained from our own past experiences and our first-hand observation of life. A married man may feel attracted to another woman, but, understanding how this desire could lead to problems and anxieties, he chooses not to act on it. This is the true meaning of renunciation which has nothing to do with escapism. You renounce an action because you know what it entails. Then you do not have to go through the unhappiness in order to learn its lesson. You can anticipate the drama before it occurs. You have been handed a script for consideration, and you decide that it is not worthy of being staged. As we grow, we tend more and more to follow the path of consciously deciding not to create dramas with unhappy consequences. Very few people, however, are strong enough and wise enough to do this all the time. With most of us the process of learning is a mixture of these two modes.

Too often we are not able to learn from the negative consequences of the dramas in which we are engaged. Instead we merely experience the conflicts and misery which accompany them. The man who was having an affair may be torn between opposing desires. Or he may be unable to make a decision, remaining worried and guilt-ridden, feeling that anything he does will make himself and others miserable. In such a situation he may seek a counselor, therapist, or spiritual guide for advice about what to do. Most people who seek counseling hope to get specific answers, specific directions for solving their problems. They often hope to get advice on how to bring about a change in those people who are "making them suffer," asking, "What should I do to make my son stop taking drugs?" or "How do I get my husband to treat me with more consideration?"

But most often the therapist will not tell you how you should relate to your son or to your spouse. He will not have any magical answers to make it all better, and if he did you probably would not follow his advice anyway. The therapist's job is to help you deal with yourself—your anxiety, fears, expectations and worries. During the course of treatment the therapist helps the patient to look more objectively at the whole situation and to disengage himself, to loosen his identification with the drama. The patient learns to see alternative roles that he might play in various situations, rather than defining himself as a rigid character with a limited script. Almost all therapists guide their patients in this direction whatever their theoretical orientation. The Rogerian therapist may lead

his client to a new sense of self-worth and self-regard;
another form of therapy may focus on helping the patient
to assume responsibility for himself; still another
emphasizes the analysis of conflicts and resistances in the
patient; but all at their core, whatever their means of
approach, help us to give up old, unproductive ways of
defining ourselves. As a result, a woman who has been in
therapy for some time might think, "In the past I always
responded with jealousy when my husband mentioned
his secretary. I have always been the jealous wife. But
I don't have to play that role any more, it's not helpful
to our relationship. I can relate differently." And so
she learns to stand back, watch the drama unfold, and
to become her own script writer, controlling rather than
being controlled by the circumstances of her life.

The process of giving up unrewarding roles is not a
one-time happening. To the extent that growth occurs
the pattern is repeated, renewing itself again and again.
For growth means redefining ourselves. Each time we
develop psychologically, a process of disidentifying and
then forming a new more inclusive identity takes place.
As new problems and conflicts arise, we may not be able
to maintain our nonidentified position and we may again
seek out a teacher who will help us to disengage from the
drama.

Each time we break free of an identification that was
part of a certain drama, our tendency is not to remain
free and open to the infinite possibilities of characters
and roles we might play but to choose a new identification
for ourselves, to become "stuck" once again. The new
character that we choose may be much more flexible

and encompassing than our previous one, but to the extent that we become attached to it we are once again closed off from further growth. We tend to get caught up in the values, goals, successes and disappointments of the new identity.

Each time we lose our perspective we experience distress, frustration and other painful emotions. During those unhappy periods when we feel unable to cope, we are the most open to new growth. For it is at such times that we look for a therapist or a spiritual guide. In this sense our most difficult and painful moments can be the most beneficial.

Since the way in which we grow psychologically and spiritually is through learning to disengage from our narrow definitions of ourselves, any therapeutic method which leads to growth, be it secular or religious, will be based on this principle. Those who come to a meditation teacher may also be seeking a shortcut to making everything all right. They may be looking for someone to give them a technique or something to believe in. Some people take up meditation in search of some easy method, a trick that will help them remain the way they are and yet no longer be unhappy. But techniques will always prove incomplete. In the end we will find that we must slowly transform our entire understanding of ourselves and the world we live in, that we must gradually learn to experience everything in a new way if we are truly to expand our consciousness and leave our unhappiness behind.

The Western psychotherapist and the meditation teacher both teach us to give up faulty identifications;

they do not differ in this respect. But there is a difference in the degree to which they take this teaching. The therapist is typically satisfied if we can disengage from our most upsetting melodramas and our major conflicts. But the spiritual guide leads us to resolve even the most subtle disturbances. If we follow the path of meditation or of a spiritual tradition, we are led beyond the initial techniques to a deeper and more profound understanding of who and what we really are behind the roles and identifications in which we have become absorbed. After helping the student to perceive the more obvious dramas in which he has become caught up, the teacher will lead him to those which are more subtle and may have gone unnoticed, including those melodramas which take place purely within our own thinking process. Gradually the student will be led beyond all the dramas to the very essence of his being.

The spiritual guide leads us to see the insubstantial nature of our dramas and to learn not to take them all so seriously. He leads us to ask what is behind all this. What lies behind the sets and the characters who pose and strut about? If you are with a master for some time, you will see a person who is flexible and who has a playful attitude toward life. He is open to playing a number of possible roles and being many different characters. You may be surprised at how changeable such a master is and how many personalities he is able to assume as the situation calls for it. He relates to his students in terms of what they need in order to give up their limited identity, their preconceived ideas and their expectations.

Most therapists limit their work to the confines of

their office at strictly appointed times. Therapy often consists of verbalizations about what has gone on in the past. A few therapists who use the technique of "psycho-drama" may stage an imagined scene to help a person see the misery-causing roles he habitually plays and how to change them. But a spiritual teacher seeing that all life is drama for the purpose of growth is more likely to stage "real life" dramas in order to bring out and correct disturbances in his students. Because of the greater sense of "reality" these learning experiences are usually extremely impactful.

Interpersonal Relations

It is important now to consider the implications of this concept of disidentification, for our relations with others. One may have the idea that learning not to take the drama of life so seriously and developing the capacity to stand apart from one's role might lead to indifferent, egocentric or irresponsible behavior. This, however, is an erroneous notion, for disidentification teaches us how to play our roles well and how to enjoy them without being caught up by the frustration and misery that is usually part of the drama.

Disidentification can actually help us in relating to other people. Normally many of us are so caught up in the drama of our life that we are constantly concerned about what others think of us. We worry about fulfilling what is expected of us by our families, friends, and associates. All these expectations create for us a certain self-image, a character with which we identify. This may be a rebellious or compliant character, but in either case we are no longer capable of free response. We act not in accordance with what we *want* to do but in accordance with what we feel we *have* to do.

Thus the role which has been molded for us begins to dominate us, and we go through life feeling that there are nothing but obligations all along the way. But if we realize the play-like quality of our situation and get free from the burden of concern over what others expect of us, our sense of "having to" can be left behind. There will no longer be a need to be compliant or rebellious, and we can start playing our roles as we see fit, without being caught up in them.

Then each role becomes for us an instrument for productive action. We can actually begin to fulfill others' expectations as a matter of free choice. At this stage we can handle all our duties without resentment and do what other people need or want of us without a sense of being exploited. With this attitude our interpersonal relations become more rewarding and more constructive. When you have disengaged from your involvement in expectations and desires, you can relate to others with much more patience, objectivity and playfulness. You can help another person when you are not caught up in your own turmoil and reactions. Then you are not swayed off balance but are able to deal with a difficult situation calmly and in a more neutral way.

A decrease in your emotional involvement does not mean a decrease in your effectiveness. On the contrary, your effectiveness is increased. Many people think that yoga and meditation imply passivity, withdrawing from the world and not caring about others, but actually quite the opposite is true. In learning disidentification we stop being anxious and overly concerned, but considerate and committed action still remains. In fact, it becomes more and more pronounced as we become less disturbed and anxious about ourselves.

When we develop a more neutral attitude and become less identified with our role, then we really open ourselves to being able to see how other people are experiencing the world. If someone in your family or a friend comes to you with a problem, you can really emphathize with him as well as take an objective stance in order to help him find a solution. You are not tied into any particular point of view based on your own egocentric involvement in that drama. So if, for example, an unmarried daughter comes to you announcing that she is pregnant, you can fully understand her feelings and try to help her solve her dilemma in the best possible way, instead of wasting your energy on negative emotions and reacting out of your own subjective fears and disappointments.

Non-attachment, not overly identifying with your own role, opens you up to seeing clearly the roles that other people are playing. Having a lot more flexibility, you can easily take another person's perspective. People no longer have as great an impact on you as before in terms of making you emotionally upset, but this is precisely what increases your perceptiveness and understanding of others.

It is important here to clarify the distinction between emotionality and a deeper sense of empathy. When someone comes to you with a problem and is expressing an intense emotion, you may think that in helping them you should also act emotional. We tend to think that this emotionality is a sign of our concern and a way of showing someone we love that we also feel their grief, anger or anxiety. However, this is only an external bond and is not likely to be beneficial in the long run. For real compassion, real understanding and real strength can be given only by a person who is inwardly centered and at peace with himself.

The Family Drama

The child is typically identified with his family, but as he moves into adolescence, he begins to question his parents' values and way of life. As adolescents and even as adults, we often experience intense conflicts between our own desires and parental expectations. This is one of the major concerns in young people who seek out psychotherapy. They may come to a therapist saying: "My mother and father want me to go to college but I have no interest in school. If I don't go they'll be disappointed in me, but if I do, I'll be unhappy. I don't know what to do. They want me to dress a certain way, to trim my hair and to do all the things *they* think are right. I feel like moving somewhere else where I can be on my own."

We usually end up with one of two responses to this situation. Some of us rebel and do the opposite of what is expected. Left to our own decisions we might complete school. But because we feel that we would not "own" that accomplishment, that we have been taken over by someone else, we staunchly reject the path suggested to us. Others of us choose to give in and go along with what the parents want. Outwardly we seem compliant but deep inside we may feel "I'm doing it for them because I have to." We strongly resent the feeling of obligation. Many of us vacillate between these two reactions.

Almost everyone experiences such conflicts to some extent. We worry over what our parents expect of us, and how to relate to those expectations. We wonder how to become free and "be ourselves." How can we respect our parents' wishes but at the same time be what we want to be? This seems impossible to most of us. But if we learn to see this situation as one of the major dramas to be played out in our life and avoid being caught up in and identifying with our part, it is possible to transform such a situation from one of conflict and strife to one of joy and harmony.

Let us give you an example of how this process works. A student described his relationship with his family in the following way: *As I was growing up I had the feeling that my parents expected a great deal from me. I was the first child and they wanted me to be the success of the family, to take care of them and through my success give them a sense of security. I was free to be a doctor, a lawyer or a businessman, so long as I was "successful." All through my adolescence I was aware of these expectations, and I rebelled against them. I never wanted to take any kind of position where I would be an authority, or would be first in achievement. Often I would wind up second best. I always reacted against their expectations that I would come out on top.*

Since becoming involved with yoga and meditation

KEY

and studying yoga psychology, my attitude has changed drastically. Instead of being bound up in others' expectations I began to gain some perspective on myself. I realized that I did not have to become caught up in the roles my parents were prescribing for me, either trying to fulfill them or rebelling against them. What was wanted from me did not seem to be such a big and important thing in defining myself, because I realized that I was distinct from the part. I could play my part without being stuck, thinking, "that's who I am."

When this new attitude really began to sink in, something strange happened. Instead of becoming less interested in my parents I found that I was able to look at them with a new openness and to see what their needs really were, rather than being caught up in my own resentments. Instead of worrying about how demanding and unfair my parents were being to me, I was able to look at the whole situation from their point of view and to think about how I could share myself with them. I could now see my parents as human beings in the parental role, with both weaknesses and positive qualities, like all of us. Rather than viewing them as supreme authorities, I realized that they had parents too, and that their parents had certain expectations of them that they are still trying to cope with. I began to think about how I could help them feel more secure and more comfortable. It then became very easy to play out my role and to fulfill their expectations in that role without myself becoming caught by it and taking it so seriously.

At that point our whole relationship changed. What before had been a pretty negative relationship turned into something very positive and beautiful. It was just this little change in my attitude that did the trick. Getting out of the framework of reacting to my parents' expectations made all the difference. When that happened, the sense of having to fulfill what was expected of me or to rebel against it dissolved, and the roles and expectations became important in a new way, in the context of my wanting to be useful and giving.

We can see from this description that being free and committed in life's play can actually lead one to carry out one's actions more perfectly and more completely than was otherwise possible, rather than cause an attitude of cold and destructive non-involvement or compliant submissiveness. A great many young people are confused in finding the way for themselves and do not know what they are doing. Thus they waste time, energy, and the best period of life which they have at their disposal. But as time passes the sense of duty grows. They understand that doing one's own duty is the only way for freedom from bondage.

The Final Drama

In this theater of life one learns to play the dual part consciously. We are all citizens of two worlds, the world within ourselves and the world outside. A skillful actor acts in such a way that he does not disturb himself in any circumstance whatsoever. To maintain peace of mind and tranquillity is the key to success in playing the drama of life.

There comes a time in life when all these petty dramas

and joys of life lose their value and the actor thinks of playing the drama with the unknown. Sometimes he finds himself afraid of the unknown and at other times dissatisfied with the known. This is a crucial point of decision. Many accept defeat, but a few determine to go ahead, to explore and unveil the reality of life. The *Isha Upanishad* says that the face of truth is hidden by the golden disc. It can be unveiled by having a one-pointed mind, courage, fearlessness, sincerity, faithfulness and truthfulness.

Just as the lamp having but a few drops of oil within wants to light with all its glamor, so does a seeker like to play this last drama of life, using all his might. The sages say that in the first step of this drama consciousness grows to the level where one says, "I am Thine," in the second stage, "Thou art mine," and at the last stage, "I and Thou are one." Then this scene drops and the actor attains the highest inexplicable joy.

Actually we all have come to play this drama, and to arrive at that day when we find one unity in diversity. Then we will see that it is only One who is playing the drama. This universe is His theater. All that which is going on in the visible and invisible world is a drama played by the only One for His own joy. One who realizes this truth becomes a witness to and enjoys the play and drama of life.

5

The Self

Like two birds of golden plumage, inseparable companions, individual self and the immortal Self are perched on the branches of the self-same tree. The former tastes of the sweet and bitter fruits of the tree; the latter, tasting of neither, calmly observes.

The individual self (*jiva*), deluded by forgetfulness of his identity with the divine Self, bewildered by his ego, grieves and is sad. But when he recognizes his own true Self, and beholds his glory, he grieves no more.

Mundaka Upanishad

As ancient psychologists pondered over the problems of life, so is the case with modern psychologists. Social psychologists today recognize how important role playing is in shaping our behavior. They sometimes stress role playing to the extent of asserting that life is nothing but a series of role enactments. Some suggest that we would be nothing if we were left without our roles. Other modern psychologists emphasize our *personality* or *character* as the major influence in determining our attitudes and ways of behaving. But this word *personality* comes from the ancient Latin word *persona* which referred to the mask used in drama. Could it be that our personality is merely a mask used to meet the outside world, and to interact with others in the drama of life? If so, who is wearing this mask?

We generally do not realize the implications inherent in the very words we use. We fail to consider that there might be someone or something behind our mask or the character we portray in life, an underlying entity who is acting out the drama.* Yoga psychology points out that there is a basic integrating force known as the Self or *Atman* which is behind all the masks we may wear. This Self, however, is unknown to our sense perception. It becomes known gradually in the course of an individual's development as his consciousness expands.**

The Self can only be perceived through meticulous refinement of our discriminating capacities. Modern psychology has, with rare exceptions, neither studied the Self nor even recognized its existence. Perhaps the subject is not within the realm of psychology. It's true that psychology is the science of mental life and it is also true that the Self is beyond senses and mind, so we do not blame them for this ignorance. How many physicists

* One of the ancient schools of psychology says that human personality is like an onion. If you open up all the layers there is nothing inside it. They forget that something can never come out of nothing. This view contrasts with Yoga psychology which describes that which underlies all layers of our being. Yoga psychology says that behind all these masks there is someone called Self.

** The ancient Indian scriptures known as the *Upanishads* provide perhaps the most precise and illuminating descriptions of the nature of the Self and its relationship to other aspects of our being.

two hundred years ago conceived of the existence of subatomic particles? Yet these are the building blocks of our material universe. Only when we developed great sophistication and comprehensiveness in our theories and extremely fine means of measuring did we become aware of these particles. Western psychology is still developing and is no more evolved than physics was several hundred years ago. Its focus has been on the more external aspects of our being which can be more or less directly observed or measured. Psychologists have studied the intricacies of personality and role playing in depth and have attained an understanding of how we come to develop particular personality styles and the functions served by specific role performances. But the more subtle aspects of our being have not yet been explored. In contrast, yoga psychology emphasizes looking beneath the performances and styles to discover who is taking on these various roles and characteristics.

An often used invocation from the *Upanishads* says:

> Lead us from the unreal to the real
> Lead us from darkness to light
> Lead us from mortality to immortality

This passage expresses the purpose and goal of yogic science in leading us to the consciousness of the Self which underlies all that is apparent, all that is impermanent. In the perennial psychology of the *Upanishads*, awareness which is enmeshed in the drama of everyday existence, is bound up in what is essentially unreal, while the Self is regarded as real and immortal because it is unchanging. All of the things we ordinarily experience go through a process of change and dissolution.

They are like dreams which dissolve when we awake, like mirages that disappear when we scrutinize them more closely with the light of awareness. The invocation is used to introduce those direct experiences which help to lead us from identification with the illusory world of ever shifting thoughts and desires to a realization of that which underlies the changing and perishable forms. Awareness of the abiding Self gives us a sense of tranquility and peace.

Without awareness of the Self, our life has no anchor or lasting meaning. We drift along in confusion desiring now one thing and then another. We are attracted to whatever is the allurement of the moment, but there is no singleness of purpose, no conception of the underlying force that guides our lives. As awareness of the Self awakens, our life takes on a new organization. Although we may at times forget and continue in old habits of drifting about from one attraction to another, we begin to come back from these side roads to a home base. As we experience the comfort of this home again and again, we return to it more and more frequently and wander about less and less. Our growth and evolution consists of realizing that the Self underlies all outer forms and working toward loosening our involvement with external and passing aspects of life. Growth means attaining a larger and larger perspective which leaves behind the narrow identification with a particular role, body or personality.

Behind the Mask of Personality

The *Atharva Veda* says of the Self:

> He is eternal. He becomes new again. He is a woman as well as a man. He is a young lady as well as a young girl. When He is old He walks taking a stick in hand and when He is born again He looks like a child in every respect. He is father as well as son. He is the eldest as well as the youngest. He is the Soul-Diety who has entered the uterus, and has become the embryo.

According to Vedantic psychology, which includes self-analysis, self-control and Self-Realization,* the Self assumes a series of outer forms or bodies while it itself remains eternal and changeless. The various experiences that we have, in each form that the Self takes, help our consciousness become more and more encompassing. We experience things from many different perspectives; and each time we become involved in a particular drama, we find out that the involvement does not bring us full contentment. As we experience the unhappiness which arises from a particular role and personality, we learn to detach ourselves from the attitudes, feelings and beliefs that go with that particular role. Each time this happens, we come closer and closer to awareness of our underlying Self. But this is a long process and it requires undergoing an almost uncountable number of melodramas.

Growing up in America, I** learned to believe that our contemporary Western knowledge of the world was the

---

* Here self refers to personality, while Self refers to the underlying essence of our being.
** Swami Ajaya

most advanced and sophisticated that man has ever possessed. When I first encountered the idea that the Self can take on a series of successive bodies it seemed to me an alien notion which I was not able to take seriously and examine objectively. I was so identified with my body that looking at my existence from any other perspective was not possible. Being familiar with Freudian psychology, I could easily pass off the belief in reincarnation as just one more defense that religions provided in order for us to pretend that our personal demise would not come about. The whole idea struck me as a primitive belief that had developed in the less sophisticated Eastern cultures. People who were not very knowledgeable or educated might believe in reincarnation, but we in the West, with our scientific approach, know better, or so I thought.

I tell you this bit of personal history because I know that many of you reading this had or now have similar reactions. Our deep-rooted convictions, aversions and material-mindedness have prevented many of us from any clear and open-minded awareness of what happens to us after we leave this physical world. Ancient psychology says that man is afraid of the unknown and that is why we do not want to examine this question. Our notions on these questions are primarily based upon fears and rationalizations formed by our long tradition and cultural living and we are reluctant to reopen this area to a fair investigation. Since most of us are identified with our egos and our bodies, we are afraid that everything ceases to exist when we lose our physical body. Our typical defense is to avoid the issue, to look aside. A consideration of the dying process and its consequences is beyond our tolerance.

We have religions and they are good. But we lack a definite philosophy of life which can give us freedom from fear. Fear of death has been obsessing the entire Western world. Organized religions, in fact, increase this fear, for they don't adequately explain the deeper spiritual teachings about the nature of life and death. Our religions are dualistic; hence fear comes. We think, "I am separated from God; I am a sinner; I am possessed by the devil. How can I get rid of the devil?" These ideas are accepted by us and we do not get an opportunity to understand the reality of life. We need a sound philosophy which has its basis in logic and is divorced from religion, if we are to really resolve these misconceptions and overcome our fears.

We remain obsessed with the fear of death and out of this fear we avoid consciously answering certain basic questions about life and death. But these questions remain in our unconscious and the unconscious provides stronger motivation than the conscious part of the mind. Solving a problem or finding an answer for such questions rather than avoiding them is the right remedy. A few vital questions, if they remain repressed in our unconscious, can create a serious problem in our behavior. Human behavior remains unsteady and uncreative without solving the basic problems of life. And death is perhaps the most important area of human experience to be understood.

How we live depends on how we conceive of what happens to us with the dissolution of our physical body. Much of our lifestyle, our deepest feelings, hopes and worries are based on conscious or unconscious notions as to what happens to us after death. The very basis of our identity, the definition of who and what we think we are, is built upon how we resolve this issue in our mind. The individual who feels that his being ends with the cessation of functioning of his material body has a very different self-image from the one who feels that the essence of his being is spiritual and will reside permanently in heaven or hell. Still, an entirely different self-concept will develop if one believes that one will exist through several lifetimes and several bodies.

Since my first sceptical reaction to the concept of reincarnation, I have begun to discover that, in many areas, the Eastern understanding of the basic laws of the universe is often more sophisticated than ours in the West. In psychology, medicine, and philosophy I have encountered a subtlety which is rare in our modern approach. With a new refined sense of Eastern cultures I began to re-examine the concept of rebirth, attempting to think about it with a less prejudicial mind and in more depth. And I gradually began to realize that it was not a primitive, naive or spooky notion at all. Instead, it comes from purely illumined experiences of the great sages and provides a subtle explanation of the nature of our being, with profound implications for the meaning of our lives. It gives us a coherent understanding of the source of good and evil in our experience as well as an explanation of why we are born into particular circumstances. It provides a comprehensive framework for understanding who and what we are beyond our mortal physical existence.

When we realize the permanence of the underlying Self we develop a fearlessness, a great courage, for we know that nothing can affect or destroy us. There is really nothing that can happen to the underlying foundation of our being. The *Bhagavad Gita* says:

> Weapons cannot cut the Self and fire cannot burn it. Untouched is the Self by drenching waters, untouched is it by parched winds.
> Beyond the power of sword and fire, beyond the powers of waters and winds, the Self is everlasting, omnipresent, never changing, never moving, ever one.

Awareness of the Self leads us to have less anxiety about our lives. We begin to have a greater sense of assurance. We gain mastery over the fear of death, and no longer try to make what is impermanent—our name, physical body and narrow self-image—into something that is eternal. The frenzied desire to perpetuate ourselves through our children, or through creating organizations, foundations and other monuments disappears. For we realize that we are more abiding than any of these. We become less concerned about lineage, whether our ancesters were German, Scandinavian or French. Most people use such facts to define themselves and to establish their identities. But when you realize that you are a traveler who is merely resting in this body and in this particular circumstance you begin to feel that ancestry and family history are not basic to defining you. You do not have to live out the values of a particular clan or nationality, for you are not limited to any such groups. Your affiliation with them is only one tiny part of your great being. To identify only with that little part would be as absurd as thinking that you are your big toe and ignoring the rest of the body.

Modern psychology's interpretation of how we come to

be the way we are is focused on environmental and parental influences in childhood and on the process of our external growth. Many psychologists have regarded the human mind at birth as a "blank slate" upon which the environment imprints its designs. Other psychologists have emphasized the importance of inherited physiological characteristics in determining our mental and psychological traits.

Yoga psychology offers still another hypothesis to help explain the origin and development of individual differences in personality. This point of view suggests that each individual comes into the world with an enormous set of predispositions which had been developed through innumerable previous experiences. According to yoga psychology, the unconscious mind remains along with the Self after the body has been left behind and takes on a series of outward forms until the light of consciousness grows to such an extent that nothing remains unconscious. That formerly tiny consciousness of individuality has then expanded to become identical with the all-encompassing consciousness of the Self.

On any given morning, you awaken into a familiar environment. You find yourself once again in your own home. In the course of the day you meet those friends, acquaintances and family members you left behind the previous day. The person which you are upon awakening is not completely new. It is a carry-over from the personality that went to sleep the night before. Your tendency to think and behave in a certain way, your particular abilities, your knowledge and skills in certain areas, all return when you open your eyes and begin your new day. So it is with the infant, from the perspective of yoga psychology. He carries with him certain tendencies and abilities, and finds himself being born into that environment which provides a continuation of his previous development.

Despite what Western psychology teaches us about the overriding importance of family influence, those of us who have observed young children are immediately struck by the great differences between one child and another within the same family. Psychologists try to account for this through differences in body, brain or genetic inheritance and then also suggest that the family environment is never quite the same for any two children. However, those who are around children find that the differences between siblings is often so great that the aforementioned factors, important as they may be, never seem to quite account for the observable facts. Even an infant who has not yet been subjected to much family influence already may show striking differences from the way its brothers and sisters behaved at the same stage of development. The notion that the child may bring its own innate tendencies into its present birth seems to fit the facts more closely, although it certainly runs directly into the prejudices of most Westerners and is quickly rejected on that account.

The importance we typically attach to the way in which we shape the child's environment or to the qualities the child inherits from us (she takes after her mother) rather than the child's own inherent characteristics seems to reflect our egocentric viewpoint in which we believe that the child is an extension of ourselves, rather than a being in its own right. Most of the parents express themselves through their children and thus suppress their individual growth, and children also form the habit of identifying themselves with their parents. This has been one of the biggest hindrances in the process of learning. If parents learn to allow the children to develop their own creative potentials, this will affect many aspects of our society and even lead to more discovery in all branches of science, psychology, art and philosophy.

Understanding our essence as Self can completely change the way parents look upon and relate to their children. Instead of seeing the child as an extension of themselves and of their own identities, they are more likely to look upon the child as an individual who has come to them with his own separate history and unique personality. Rather than feel that they must influence the child, they might be more inclined to see themselves as working with the unique circumstances, knowledge and attitudes that the child brings to them. The parents can then try to make the way more clear and easy for him in fulfilling his potential and developing along his own evolutionary path. If such were the parents' attitude, there would be less attachment to the child, less of the idea of molding him to their own image. There would be less of a feeling that the child's behavior reflects upon the parents and less dependency on the child to fulfill and carry on the parents' line. A sense of possessiveness would greatly diminish. All in all, an understanding of the idea of Self would be highly beneficial for family life. Relationships that were formerly filled with conflict, manipulation and strife would become more open, nurturing and harmonious.

Two Concepts of Development

The Self remains ever the same. Here we find a difference between the Eastern and Western understanding of our essential being. In Western spiritual traditions the soul is often understood as something which undergoes change. But in the Eastern conception of the Self there is no change. The Self is an eternal center of consciousness and the growth process is merely the gradual realization that, as the ancient scriptures say: "THOU ART THAT," we are indeed the Self.

All the Western religions have dualistic philosophies in which it is said that the soul is subordinate to the absolute;   while in Eastern philosophy the Self is omnipresent and omnipotent and the individual soul has no separate existence of its own. Because of *maya* (cosmic illusion), the individual soul appears to separate itself and thus suffers, but after Self-Realization the individual self and cosmic Self are one and the same. Of all the various schools of philosophy, the most highly evolved is Shankara's school, which teaches that there is one and only one absolute without a second and "THOU ART THAT." Shankara says, "it is ignorance that causes us to identify with the body, the ego, the senses or anything that is not the Self."*

The Self remains everlasting while all about there is multiplicity and change. The *Isha Upanishad* states: "To the ignorant the Self appears to move—yet it moves not."

---

*   Aldous Huxley, *The Perennial Philosophy*, Chatto & Windus, London, 1946, p. 13.

From the point of view of Eastern psychology then, all that undergoes change is merely a covering to the Self. Even our physical body is nothing but a garment, which through time becomes old and tattered, and which eventually must be discarded and replaced by a new one. The Self remains unchanging, but the outer manifestations which hide it now take this form and now that.

In yoga psychology and philosophy, the path of individual development is made up of the gradual uncovering of this Self that lies hidden at the center of our being. The way we work on ourselves as we expand our awareness is much the same as that of a sculptor who works on a block of marble. He chips away all the superfluous material to reveal a beautiful form within. As we grow, we cast off those objects, concepts, thoughts and memories which had surrounded and obscured our essential being.

There is a marked contrast in the conception of the growth process in the East and in the West. The preconceptions inherent in the Western understanding of the soul (that it is distinct from the absolute and subject to change) remains with us in modern psychology's understanding of human development. While in the East development is an uncovering of that perfection which is already there, the Western concept of growth tends to imply a building-up process. The course of development is seen as a molding and shaping of ourselves until we form a particular personality, set of habit patterns, and attachments which we define as "I." In the Eastern tradition, all of this is considered superficial and a misconception of who we are, for it puts the emphasis and focus of attention on the extraneous marble which is to be chiseled away and discarded.

Thus there is a fundamental difference between these two traditions in conceiving of our basic nature, in who and what we really are. This is reflected in our concepts of identification and identity. In Eastern psychology it is the Self, or pure consciousness, which identifies itself with the thoughts, desires, and external stimuli that come to the attention of the mind, whereas in Western psychology, the personality is taken for granted as the basis of who we are. In Western psychology it is the personality of the individual that identifies itself with others, with objects and possessions. It is not seen as that excess stone to be removed but as the very foundation of our being, since there is nothing underneath, nothing hidden within, nothing else.

In Eastern psychology our real and essential identity can only be the Self—all other identities are misconceptions of who and what we are. But in modern psychology our identity is defined in terms of external events, behaviors, possessions and attachments. Thus in the Western conception of growth and development and in the Western practice of psychotherapy there is little appreciation of the fact that we can go beyond such identifications without becoming disorganized or regressing. Modern psychotherapy may help a person *replace* a disabling self-concept with one that leads to greater adjustment and satisfaction, but it typically stops when this is achieved. Yoga psychology as a therapeutic process carries the individual further to help him *give up* all of those attachments, addictions and identifications which he has with the more superficial layer of his being.

Self-awareness is attained only after a slow and deliberate process of consciousness expansion. There are many distractions along the way in this long and difficult journey. We frequently stop to enjoy the enticement of the moment or become absorbed in our attachment to a particular melodrama, forgetting the purpose of our travels. But, according to Yoga psychology, each of us is bound eventually to reach awareness of the Self, however distracted we may temporarily become. We wander about in the world looking for fulfillment, completeness, a sense of being at home. We seek this sense of completeness through companions, in possessions, and in new adventures and experiences, but finally we come away disappointed, for completeness can only be found deep within. We look under one rock and then another to find what is missing in us, never realizing that what we are really seeking is close at hand, never realizing that we already have it but are keeping it hidden from our awareness. In the *Isha Upanishad* it is said: "From the ignorant the Self is far distant—yet it is near." For, though the Self is the core of our being, psychologically we are separated from it by the huge cavern of our fantasies, illusions and false concepts about ourselves. There is a wonderful story which illustrates this relationship between the Self and our more limited consciousness:

> Two children lived with their mother on the outskirts of a high mountain village. The children had never met their father. They had an intense desire to be united with him. They pleaded with their mother to take them to see him,

but she kept putting them off. She told them that it would not be easy to reach their father. They would have to cross over several mountain ranges, and through deep forests. There would be many precarious rivers in their path which would be difficult to cross.

But the children were so intent on being with their father that day after day they asked when they could begin their journey. Seeing the intensity of the children's desire, the mother could resist no longer. "We will start when we have properly prepared ourselves," she said, "when we have the proper provisions, food and warm clothing, when we are physically and mentally ready for the hardships we will face, then we will go." They all worked diligently to prepare. They lived more austerely, giving up many small pleasures in order to obtain the necessary provisions, but they found an even greater joy in what they were accomplishing together. Finally when the day came for them to depart the children were overjoyed.

For the next several months they endured many hardships. They were often exhausted or hungry, but they persevered. They traveled hundreds of miles on foot over difficult terrain. At last they came to a plateau that looked vaguely familiar. Pointing to a house in the distance, the mother said, "that is where your father lives, now you will meet him." The children could hardly believe that they had almost arrived at their longed for goal. As they approached the house and knocked on the door, they could hardly stand the anticipation.

When their father came out, he was as overjoyed as the children. He took them in his arms and brought them inside. where they played together through the day, singing, dancing, telling stories, and being at home. He had many presents to give them. Later as the sun was setting, the children became sleepy. Their father pointed to a door, telling them that in the next room they would find warm, comfortable beds. Tired but content, the children opened the door. When they went into the next room they were surprised to find that they were in their own house, and that their father had been living unseen, right next to them all the time.

Our Self is always with us, but only through sacrificing our more limited attachments, and traversing a long and circuitous route in which we gain mastery over the more superficial aspects of our being, can we return home and become united with that source of fulfillment.

According to the well–known schools of Eastern psychology, analyzing and really understanding the word "Self" involves a great deal of time and effort. In the ancient scriptures *Atman* and *Brahman* are often used in describing the Self. The "Real-Self" and "mere-self," the "Higher-Self" and "lower-self," these words are defined clearly by the *Upanishads, Brahma Sutras* and the *Bhagavad Gita.* The entire Vedantic psychology stands on the distinction between the Real-Self and the mere-self, that which is *Atman* and that which is not.

This simple diagram will help the reader in understanding this distinction more clearly.

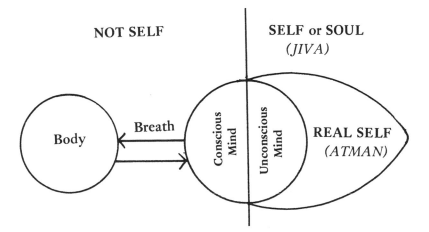

According to Vedantic psychology the body, breath and conscious mind are distinguished from the Self because they are impermanent and are left behind at the time of death. The Real Self and the unconscious mind remain. The unconscious is the storehouse of past impressions (memories). As long as one remains identified with the impressions in the unconscious mind he must return again to the world in order to bring the latent desires and identifications to fruition and experience their effects. Through this process these identifications are dissolved and one realizes his identity as the Self or pure consciousness without the limitations of any personal history. Since the unconscious remains with the Real Self through the course of evolution until the final stage when all becomes conscious, these two together are sometimes referred to as the individual-self, *jiva*, or in Western terminology, the soul. This is to be distinguished, however, from the Real Self, *Atman*, or *Brahman* which remains after all else is left behind.

The process of seeking and the attainment of perfection are two different stages. A student who is still treading the path wants to know the mere-self or the world, that which apparently exists for him; but he also wants to know that underlying reality which remains witnessing above all the changes of this universe. These two seem to be distinct. When one studies the *Upanishads* under the guidance of his spiritual teacher he finds a practical difficulty in understanding a few contradictions which are found there, such as:

This is all *Brahman.*
Brahman alone is truth and all else is false.
There is only one Absolute without a second.

Those who study these texts without the help of a competent teacher can never understand these gems of truth which come from the source of direct knowledge. A teacher first teaches a student to be very practical in understanding that which is Self and that which is not-self. When one practices truth with mind, action and speech, then he can never see not-self, but only one Real Self. When one has known the ultimate truth or the Real Self, for such a one, not-self also becomes *Brahman.* Verily this is all *Brahman.*

6

Freedom and Responsibility

In the Godhead itself, the most *perfect freedom* and the most absolute necessity are joined together in a Marriage, to which the whole Heavens and Earth, with unutterable joy sing eternal Marriage-Songs.

Peter Stery

Homer prayed for peace and harmony. Heraclitus said they are not possible because of the two diverse principles which are seen in such dualities as happiness and grief, joy and sorrow, and freedom and bondage. But Tagore went a step forward and said, "Oh Lord, let me have the inner strength which will help me in going through all the trials and turbulence of life. Let me rise above these limiting dualities." Freedom is often misunderstood. For a child, freedom may mean doing what he wants irresponsibly. But can we really call this freedom? Human life seems to be enveloped by pain, miseries and bondage. Real emancipation comes after understanding the bondage of this life and transcending it. In the East such freedom may be called *moksha* or *nirvana.* A human being is not born freed, but can attain freedom by sincere efforts.

We have seen how the expansion of consciousness leads us to free ourselves from the identities which we once took so seriously. As we become aware of the Self, we take on a less rigid, more playful attitude toward what we may think and do. But this newly found freedom from the confinement of identifying ourselves with our personality and thoughts does not bring with it license to behave in any manner we may choose. Instead, it enables us to perceive a more subtle order to our existence and to act in accordance with it rather than blindly follow prescriptions or beliefs based on narrow self-definitions. We become able to perceive a more profound order which is established not by human institutions, but by nature itself.

The lawfulness which reveals itself to us when we are no longer preoccupied with more superficial codes of conduct in the drama of life is found to transcend culture, customs and traditions. It provides a lasting and coherent groundwork for guiding our lives. We begin to see that by living in harmony with this order we create a sense of harmony within ourselves, and that when we ignore, disdain or try to avoid recognizing the natural order, we experience misery and unhappiness. Our understanding of the law of gravity, the speed at which light travels, and numerous other aspects of the organization of our environment help us live more effectively in the physical world. Similarly, the understanding of the psychological aspect of nature's order can help us live more fully in the mental, emotional and spiritual realms.

The lawful working of this natural order has been expounded to us by spiritual teachers throughout the ages. These guides have in many cases achieved a profound understanding of our psychological and spiritual makeup. All too often we have failed to perceive their teachings as the explication of natural law and have, instead, taken them to be just another set of rigid prescriptions and rules. But actually the teachings of the masters are as firmly based on the order of nature as is modern science. One of the most basic of the psychological laws which has been revealed to us is the law of freedom and responsibility, which states that freedom and responsibility exist in direct proportion to each other. They are so much mingled that they cannot be separated; lawlessness is not freedom, but lawfulness can be.

Misconceptions About Freedom

Freedom is an experience that in our culture is regarded as being extremely important. We value freedom perhaps more than any other state, and yet many of us have confused or mistaken notions about it. Most people think that freedom is something that is given to them by others. We feel that freedom is something that is due us, an "inalienable right" that should be granted to us on demand. "This is a free country," we say, implying that we have the right to do whatever we like.

In our experiences at correctional institutions we find the prisoners preoccupied with the attainment of their freedom from incarceration. Their thoughts are centered on the day when they will be let out. Their predominant concern is with how to convince the parole board that their freedom should be handed to them. They have little conception of how freedom may be attained by their own efforts. How many of us are ourselves like this! We desire to be free from obligations, from unhappiness, from physical suffering, and all too often we look toward others to release us. Perhaps we may pray for deliverance, or hope that a doctor can cure us of the misery that besets our bodies, while all along we continue to abuse ourselves.

Despite our conviction that we are a free nation, that we have freedom of choice, each one of us upon careful examination will find that we are, in fact, slaves to our emotions, to irrational impulses, to habits, and to desires for sensual pleasure and comfort. We are entrapped in the drama of our existence, and all the while we mock ourselves with the protest that we are free individuals. The recognition of our enslavement to addictions, to comforts, to people who can bolster our low spirits, need not lead us to become pessimistic. For freedom from all these encumbrances can truly be attained. However, in order to gain this freedom we must first of all give up the illusion that freedom may come to us from an external source. We must face our enslavement squarely and begin to work slowly to untie the knot through our own efforts.

Inseparability of Freedom and Responsibility

You have merely to observe the way in which nature functions to understand how to achieve freedom from all of the fetters that bind you. Whether you watch the development of a child, the way in which society deals with criminals, or your control over your body, you will see one common process. Whenever there is an increase in freedom there is also a corresponding increase in personal responsibility; that freedom only exists in the context of responsibility. It does not make sense to talk about freedom alone, for the two, freedom and responsibility, always go hand in hand and one cannot exist without the other. We will find that the whole of our natural world is arranged in this way, that freedom exists only in proportion to the amount of responsibility that we assume.

Let us look at the development of freedom in a child. When a child is very young, the parents assume full responsibility, leaving him very little freedom of choice. The parent selects the food the child will eat and puts him down for a nap at a chosen time despite his protests. If a toddler wishes to go outside and play, his area of movement will be restricted. Mother may choose to allow him outside only when she is there to watch, or she may confine him to a securely fenced-in yard.

The child does not yet have enough responsibility to take care of itself. If allowed to play on the front lawn, it could become so emotionally caught up in the moment that it might chase the ball out into the street without heeding the traffic. So, if you have a three-year-old daughter who wants to go out and play on the sidewalk, you would be reluctant to allow her that freedom. Though she might protest and become upset at the restrictions you place upon her, you realize that these restrictions are necessary in view of her immaturity and inability to prevent herself from being injured.

As the child becomes older and more self-reliant, the parent begins to relinquish control and, as a result, the child gains greater freedom. At one time Mother may have said, "You can't go outside unless Mommy is with you." Later, the child may be allowed to play in the fenced-in back yard alone, and, as the child matures further, Mother may allow her to play on the front lawn. But she will still restrict her activities to the edge of the sidewalk. Crossing the street to play with the neighbors must not be done without supervision. As the child grows, so do her cognitive capacities and awareness. The mother realizes that she is now able to look up and down the street, to watch for cars, and to understand the danger of being hit by a car. She may look out the window as her daughter is allowed to cross the street alone for the first few times, making sure that the necessary caution is taken. When reassured, the mother will relinquish responsibility in this area to her child. Thus the child acquires a greater range of movement and becomes open to a wider realm of experience in venturing about the neighborhood.

When this child reaches the age of fifteen there are still certain freedoms which have not been given to her. She is not yet free to drive a car, to vote, or to buy alcohol. But when society feels that she has reached an age where she is likely to be responsible enough in handling the increased freedom, the privileges are granted. Then the youngster can travel about unrestrictedly, and soon she can even participate in electing those who will determine the laws that deal with shared freedoms and responsibilities. This gradual process of gaining more and more freedom along with the development of self-control and responsibility continues into adulthood and beyond.

The young person may look upon freedom as something which is handed to him merely by virtue of reaching a certain age, rather than realize the extent to which freedom is dependent upon his assumption of responsibility. But if we look at the way all societies operate, we will see how they commonly follow this general principle of granting freedom only when responsibility is shown. The teenager can receive a driver's license only when he has demonstrated that he can handle the car responsibly. The mother who, looking through the window, sees her daughter crossing the street without paying attention to oncoming cars will immediately withdraw that privilege from the child. The child's freedom of movement will again become more restricted. Similarly, if an adult behaves irresponsibly, if he injures others or trespasses on their rights, freedom is withdrawn from him. His interaction with others is restricted. If he should assault someone or steal, he is likely to be confined to a prison where once again others will take responsibility for him. And he is treated in many ways like a child, like one who cannot assume responsibility for himself. Thus in the prison setting he may be provided with food, with clothing, and be under the strict supervision of authority figures who tell him when he may eat, sleep or go out for recreation. In general, whenever someone does not take responsibility for himself and cannot keep from injuring himself or others, his freedom is taken away.

We have now seen how freedom and responsibility go hand in hand as parents relate to their children, and also as societies as a whole relate to their individual members. The examples given seem to be germane to almost all times and cultures. Whenever an individual is in a position where harm may be done to himself or to others and he is not able to assume responsibility in avoiding that harm, we find an external agent stepping in and taking control. In that process freedom is necessarily restricted. Conversely, we find that as individuals demonstrate their capacity to avoid injuring themselves and others, their freedom increases. In almost all cases it seems that the degree of freedom allowed is evaluated in terms of the potential damage that might be done as freedom becomes greater.

As long as there appears to be no threat of injury, one can engage in behavior which may, perhaps, strike others as somewhat strange and unusual. Society allows people to express themselves in whatever manner they choose as long as the general order of things is not disrupted by it. As an example of this, I* am reminded of my consultation work at a maximum security psychiatric hospital. Each week, as I would come to the barred and locked entrance, the gatekeeper would open the door and greet me with a friendly though humorous comment. I was dressed in the saffron-colored Indian garb of a swami, a shawl draped over my shoulders, my hair uncut down my back and sandals on my feet. No one who was a patient in the institution dressed as uniquely and, from the officers' and patients' point of view, as strangely as I. And yet, at the end of the day,

* Swami Ajaya

the door would be opened for me to leave, while the patients whose dress seemed much more normal and acceptable to others than mine would be confined inside. For it was not the "bizarreness" of their everyday behavior that caused their freedom to be taken from them; it was instead the assaults or suicide attempts that led the court to feel that they could not behave responsibly in a less restrictive situation.

The connection between freedom and responsibility that has been described applies not only in the realm of interpersonal relations, but we can see it in operation just as clearly if we look at our physiological functioning. The way in which nature has constructed the human organism clearly indicates that freedom and responsibility go hand in hand, that one occurs only along side of the other.

There are many physiological processes which are under our conscious control. We may decide when to move our arms or legs or to stand up and sit down and, barring an accident, we can direct these functions without causing ourselves injury. But there are also many functions which cannot be so directed. Most of us cannot increase or decrease our blood pressure or heart rate at will. We cannot control many internal functions of our body such as the production of adrenalin or other hormones. Nature has provided us with internal autonomic regulators for controlling these processes and keeping them in proper adjustment.

Some of us might say that there is really no need to consciously regulate internal functions, that nature has done us a service by taking on this job so that we need not be preoccupied with complex processes such as adjusting our heart rate, hormone secretions, etc. We can free our minds to become involved with other "more important" concerns. Yet there are times when the regulation of these functions goes out of balance and, as a result, we suffer from illnesses such as high blood pressure, diabetes, obesity, sluggishness, hyper-excitability, and countless other ailments. At such times it might be quite useful for us to be able to have control over the functions which bring on these imbalances in our system. But, in most cases, we are not able to do so. We have not gained the keys to operating these mechanisms. We have not been granted this freedom. Could it be, perhaps, because we are not responsible enough to perform this vital task?

Suppose it were possible for us to regulate our heart, to speed it up or slow it down at will. Could we do so without injuring ourselves? Even in those areas where nature has given us the freedom of self-determination, we often abuse our bodies and minds. In taking amphetamines and other harmful drugs or in racing a car at over a hundred miles an hour, our ability to act volitionally puts us in danger of permanent injury or even death. Nature, like the mother looking out of the window at her child crossing the street, allows us a certain amount of freedom in which there is an element of danger But when it comes to the most vital functions which are directly responsible for preserving life, nature imposes a limit on self-determination.

If we were able, by choice, to accelerate the beat of our heart or to increase the production of a certain hormone, we might experience very pleasurable sensations. It might no longer be necessary to smoke marijuana or drink alcohol if we could get a "high" simply by readjusting our internal mechanism. But such use of our physiological regulators might do them great damage. How long could our heart function at an accelerated pace without impairment? What are the limits of that acceleration? We might be able to increase the secretion of a hormone to get a "rush," but would we ask ourselves how that might affect the rest of the body? The whim or desire of the moment might lead us to do irreparable harm to ourselves. And if we damage our brain, how shall we tread the path to higher consciousness?

A few rare individuals who have developed personal responsibility to an incredible degree have shown that they can consciously control such functions that were formerly thought to be impossible to regulate. Those masters who have undergone years of intensive yogic training have learned how to act more wisely than most of us. For example, they do not indulge in foods and stimulants which may be harmful to the body. They do not seek out experiences which would gratify their physical and psychological desires but are more concerned with finding ways to promote their general well-being as well as that of others. They become free from the bondage of desire, in addition to acquiring freedom from the instinctive and more "programmed" regulation of their bodily function. They also become free of enslavement to emotions and unproductive patterns of thinking. Their behavior is motivated by the concern for the greatest good for all rather than by the urge to enjoy immediate physical pleasures. For such individuals there is little danger that they would misuse their freedom and injure themselves as a result of seeking shortsighted gratification.

In the course of their training such yogis often learn to regulate internal functions to a degree which we would find difficult even to imagine. For instance, they are able to alter their heart rate, speeding it up, slowing it down and even stopping it without causing themselves injury.

It is the assumption of greater responsibility which allows the yogi increased freedom with respect to his body, instinctive urges, emotions and thoughts. He uses such mastery to lead him toward the experience of expanded states of consciousness. For he can leave behind the encumbrances of body, emotions and thoughts. His experiences, in contrast to those produced by drugs, are under his own conscious control. While the use of drugs for this purpose could be described as an uncontrolled "blasting" of the system, the yogi's control of vital functions helps him to achieve altered states of consciousness in a pre-directed programmed manner and enables him to continue normal functioning as he returns unharmed to ordinary states of consciousness.

The yogi's achievement of freedom is a very gradual process that may take a number of years. It is a slow and meticulous process of becoming aware of the most subtle aspects of our functioning control mechanisms which typically determine behavior and experiences, though below the realm of our awareness. Just as a child, slowly, over many months, learns to operate its limbs in order to walk, the yogi, over a much longer period of time, through trial and error and through considerable effort, learns to master all internal processes. This responsible effort eventually helps him to greatly increase his freedom, both physiologically and on the mental and spiritual levels as well.

Whereas the child learns to travel throughout the neighborhood and, as it grows more responsible, throughout the city, country and the world, the yogi learns to travel through the realms of consciousness. The whole practice of yoga is one of gaining mastery over all aspects of our lives, physical, emotional, mental and spiritual. There is a continual increase in the responsibility which is assumed. Not only does the yogi take responsibility for his actions but for his thoughts as well. As this happens, his freedom increases further and he is able to regulate his thoughts in whatever manner he pleases. He can channel his mind to specific thoughts which will lead him toward certain spiritual experiences; he can concentrate his mind on a single thought for long periods of time and thereby enter new dimensions of experiencing which have been called *nirvana*, cosmic consciousness, or *samadhi*.

As the yogi learns to perfectly control his actions, speech and thoughts for the purpose of avoiding injury toward anyone, he also acquires the ability to extend his freedom and control to the realm of nature. The many miracles that are described in the Bible are performed by those spiritual leaders who have taken responsibility for the welfare of all. When this degree of responsibility is assumed, one attains the freedom to regulate nature to achieve what is needed in discharging that responsibility.

To many of us such miracles seem remote and unbelievable. They seem to be like childish stories about Santa Claus, or myths given to us to bolster our faith. But miraculous occurrences are not confined, as many of us think, to fables or to the distant past. Mastery over nature is being demonstrated by the great masters of the world even today, although it is not shown to many. It is rare for most of us to experience such events, for we are too preoccupied with our own material desires and self-interests to bring ourselves into the proximity of such masters and such experiences. But when we begin to leave our immediate concerns behind and develop a greater and more subtle sense of responsibility toward ourselves and others, we may eventually come in contact with masters who have the freedom to regulate natural events. If we would but develop our responsibility perfectly enough, we would find that, indeed, we ourselves could have such freedom.

The reader should not suppose from this description that the achievement of power and control over oneself or over nature is a goal for which to strive. In fact, those who seek after this end for its own sake will inevitably cause themselves harm, for such power in the service of a limited self-concept would be destructive. Just as atomic energy can be extremely dangerous in the hands of an individual or group motivated solely by self-interest, so are the powers to regulate our internal or external environment. It is only when we have no ambition to gain power, when our sole interest is in the elimination of injury and in the welfare of all that the freedom to regulate internal and external processes can be enjoyed. Many people think that assuming responsibility for others can create obstacles in the path of freedom. But this is not true. Taking an increased responsibility actually frees us from the narrow preoccupations, fears and worries of our small personal "I."

As we expand our consciousness to realize our essential unity and oneness with all, we transcend the fetters of our narrow preoccupations. We begin to act in harmony with our surroundings. We become one with the divine order abiding in ever-new joy and peace which knowledge of life's unity brings. True freedom is not rebellion or emancipation from this order but living in harmony with it. It is freedom from all the narrow and false constructs we have created and which limit our experience of fulfillment. We definitely should understand this deeper meaning of the word freedom and not become caught by more narrow conceptions and interpretations of what freedom is.

Freedom as it is understood in the East and in the West is entirely different. When I studied various cultures I found a major difference between the social structures of the East and West. The Western culture believes in external freedom but the Eastern culture believes in internal freedom. A Western man can get married to anyone and build his own social structure around him. No doubt he has external freedom. But in his internal life we find constraint and conformity. For example, the various religious sects in the West have to pray through Christ alone. There doesn't seem to be internal freedom for a Western religious man. In the East it doesn't seem to work this way. Socially one cannot do what he wants, but five members in a family can live together harmoniously while they have different objects of meditation and worship. They are mentally free and socially in bondage. In the West people are socially free but mentally in bondage. This seems to be one of the subtle differences between Eastern and Western cultures.

So there are varieties of freedom. It is necessary to find out what is really limiting us and achieve freedom in that area of our lives. But we should be careful, for we often create many misconceptions about what is restricting us and do not get to the real source. In each case, freedom implies release from some bondage. We have to ask, what is the bondage from which we need release. Definitely we need freedom from pain, miseries and ignorance. The entire Buddhist literature is based on achieving freedom from all pains and miseries. The lowest level of freedom is freedom from pain but the highest is freedom from ignorance. There cannot be any wisdom unless we free ourselves from the misconceptions and false concepts which we have been carrying. The message of the sages is that we must first of all attain freedom from all fears, so that we no longer cling to the familiar but limiting ideas, habits and preoccupations which we have. With this courage we can tread the path systematically loosening the various fetters that bind us until we finally come out of our cage of ignorance and realize our true nature which knows no boundaries and no limitations.

$\underset{\mathcal{S}}{\mathcal{L}}$ 7

Emotions and Their Creative Use

When a man dwells on the pleasures of sense, attraction for them arises in him. From attraction arises desire, the lust of possession, and this leads to passion, to anger.

From passion comes confusion of mind, then loss of remembrance, the forgetting of duty. From this loss comes the ruin of reason, and the ruin of reason leads man to destruction.

But the soul that moves in the world of the senses and yet keeps the senses in harmony, free from attraction and aversion, finds rest in quietness.

In this quietness falls down the burden of all her sorrows, for when the heart has found quietness, wisdom has also found peace.

*The Bhagavad Gita**

The regulation of our emotional life is a very important aspect of the growth of consciousness. The less developed our consciousness the more we tend to become caught up in unpleasant emotional states. But as our

---

* *The Bhagavad Gita*, translated by Juan Mascaro, Penguin Books, Middlesex, England, 1962, p. 54.

awareness expands, our emotional life becomes more integrated and channeled toward the experience of more positive affects. Conflictual and unhappy emotions such as anger, jealousy, fear, depression and guilt are left behind. Instead, the energy which gave rise to these states is experienced in a more refined and purified form as joy, peace, love and compassion. Before going further in describing these emotions themselves, I would like to explain the manifestations from which various streams of emotions spring. This will help us to understand how the emotions arise.

Instinctual Urges

When Freud stressed the importance of the sexual drive as a source of our emotional life, he was not wrong. The sexual urge is definitely a very powerful urge and many of our emotional states come from this drive. But there are deeper urges than sex—urges such as food, sleep and self-preservation. According to yoga psychology, many of our emotions originate from these four inherent springs or basic instinctual urges. They exist in both animals and man and serve the purpose of insuring survival of the individual and continuance of the species. These basic and universal drives, the need for food, self-preservation, sleep and sex, lead us to (1) seek out the amount of nourishment necessary to maintain life; (2) avoid life-threatening situations and defend ourselves when threatened; (3) get the adequate rest and revitilization needed for health; and (4) seek out sexual partners to participate in the creation of new life. Without these drives we might easily perish.

The drive for self-preservation seems to be stronger than the other three urges. Food is a necessity of the body first and then of the mind; sleep is a necessity of the body and conscious mind both. Sex, though it seems to be a necessity of the body, a biological need of man, is more related to the mind. But self-preservation is the urge for which we take food, sleep and enjoy sex. This is the strongest urge.

But why does one want to live for a long time? The *Isha Upanishad* says that you should aspire to live for a hundred years at least. But living a hundred years is burdensome without knowing the purpose of life. Life is not meant just for satisfying the urges.

Desire

Between primitive urges and emotions lies the level of desires. If we analyze our behavior, we will see that many of the things that we do are based on these four basic urges and the desires that spring from them.

In animals these instinctual urges are expressed in a straight-forward fashion. An animal, when hungry, may seek out the nearest source of food that is edible, or in mating it will seek out any animal of its species which is in its proximity. Self-preservation is a relatively simple matter of warding off physical dangers or maintaining a place in the pecking order. Man, however, has used his imagination to create innumerable varieties of objects, experiences and situations to satisfy these urges. When we are hungry we are not satisfied with just any food;

most of us have developed a taste for very specific dishes. Sometimes we may even reject the food which is the most nourishing in favor of that which appeals to our various senses or even that which is more socially accepted. While in many animals the sexual urge may be satisfied with any other animal of the opposite sex, in humans the object of our satisfaction is often one particular person who is attractive because of some subtle quality which may be quite unrelated to the basic physiological instinct. We may often pass up potential partners who are in our proximity and travel hundreds of miles to seek out that particular individual with whom we feel a special affinity. The self-preservation drive has also been extended to include the desire for status, power and the accumulation of numerous possessions.

In man the basic urges have become an almost unlimited number of desires for specific experiences. We spend a great deal of our time in trying to satisfy the many desires that have grown out of these few basic urges. It is in seeking to obtain and keep objects of our desire that we become emotional in one way or another. Thus it is said that desire is the mother of all emotions.

When we obtain the satisfaction of a desire through a particular object or situation, we experience pleasure. When this becomes a habit, we become dependent on or addicted to that experience. Usually we use the word *addiction* to refer to dependencies on particular intoxicants such as alcohol or narcotics. However, if we analyze our desires for other objects, we will see that we relate to them with much the same kind of dependency. We become intoxicated with many experiences, people and objects in the world. Our addictions are much more numerous than most of us realize. We are all aware of the intense or even violent emotions that may be experienced by an addict who cannot obtain what he craves. This situation is merely an exaggerated version of experiences that bring about unpleasant emotions in all of us. The intensity of our emotions is related to how massive our addiction to a particular object is. *

How Negative Emotions Arise and are Transformed

Anger

Anger is a violent emotion without reason. Reason disappears when one gets angry. The faculty of discrimination between right and wrong does not function.

When there is a strong unfulfilled desire for an object or an experience, we usually feel angry toward whatever is keeping us from fulfilling our desire. If, for example, you want to be somewhere on time but you get into your car and it will not start, you may clench your jaws or even hit your fist against the steering wheel in anger. Or if you are driving to your destination and your way is blocked by a truck, you may be quite angry at the driver of that vehicle who is making you late. Anger also occurs when we feel invaded or injured in one way or another. If you have already attained the object you desire and you feel that it is a part of you, you may

---

* A similar analysis can also be applied to the experience of displeasure and its consequent *aversion* for certain situations or objects. The desire to avoid unpleasant experiences can also lead to unpleasant emotions.

become angry if it is taken from you. If you are attached to a new car and someone damages it, you are likely to feel angry toward that person because he is damaging something which you possess.

Many people believe that anger is useful in order to defend oneself. Such emotional arousal may be helpful at the more primitive, instinctual levels of organization where an animal must physically defend itself in the struggle for survival. But in modern man anger and other physiologically arousing emotions usually create disturbance rather than protect us. In animals or in primitive man the arousal of the autonomic nervous system in reaction to emergencies gives an increased surge of energy for fight of flight reactions. However, psychologists are finding that in our typical living situation today there is more apt to be a chronically mild arousal as we try to cope with the stresses and uncertainties of modern life. It is felt that ulcers, high blood pressure and various psychosomatic diseases have their origin in such maladaptive chronic arousal.

We typically feel that anger is a necessary component in asserting ourselves against threat, but actually this is not the case. It is possible to be forceful and dynamic and even to control someone who is aggressive toward you without yourself becoming aroused. If someone abuses you or hurts your ego, you can show him the limits of what you will tolerate. Yet it is not necessary to feel that surge of venom within yourself which comes with the activation of the autonomic nervous system and the endocrine system. You may find you can be more effective by maintaining objectivity and emotional calmness in your assertiveness than when you lose control. Several Eastern martial arts are based on this principle. In Kung Fu, Karate, Judo, Aikido, etc., it is suggested that the best way of dealing with invasion is to remain neutral and to use the invader's energy against him rather than to become emotional in retaliation. The notion that anger is an essential means of self-defense has no basis in reality.

Some people may feel that the expression of so-called "negative" emotions has a positive value for the person releasing the emotion. Those especially who have been involved in psychotherapy or encounter groups may have learned to become more sensitive to their emotions and to use them as a means of "finding themselves." Yoga psychology would agree that it is helpful to be aware of one's anger and even to release it rather than to suppress it and to pretend that it is not there. But this seems to be only a temporary remedy. In this way you do not learn how to control your emotional life and make it more creative and useful. Every violent emotion needs expression. It is bound to erupt in one way or another. But expressing emotion without learning how to utilize and channel that emotional power can be destructive to oneself and others. Emotional power is valuable, but negative emotions are not. Knowing the technique of channeling that emotional power can be very positive, for the emotional side of man provides a power that thoughts alone do not have. When this power is utilized properly in coordination with the mental life, man can do wonders. Ordinary therapists cannot teach you *where* to express the emotional thrust, but yoga psychology provides such guidance.

Jealousy

When we have a strong desire for something and our goal is blocked, we experience anger. But when someone else succeeds in attaining that object, person or experience while we cannot do the same, the feeling which usually occurs is jealousy or envy.* We enter a state of competition. We would like to imagine ourselves in the other person's shoes. If a man desires to be with a woman but is spurned by her, he may experience anger toward her for resisting him, but he will also feel jealousy if he sees another man with her.

The person who feels jealous senses a lack within himself and is focused on an external object as his source of fulfillment. He creates within his mind a psychological state of longing and disappointment, a sense that he cannot attain what he must have. The weak person is always jealous. Those who have a strong will and know how to use their reason do not become victims of this unhealthy emotion.

The *Isha Upanishad* says, "Do not covet another man's wealth." Do not become intrigued or preoccupied with what another has or seems to enjoy. If you but knew the situation better, you would find that the joy you imagine another to have is more apparent than real. When you become aware of the Self, true joy becomes abundant, and that joy, being the essence of your being, is not an object which can be snatched away by anyone else. In

* If we have attained it in the past, jealousy is felt; if we have never gotten the longed-for object or person, we feel envy.

knowing the Self within, we will realize that completeness does not come from outside. All sense of jealousy and envy will be left behind. We will know that all there is to attain is already with us, and has merely been kept from our awareness by our preoccupation with externals.

Fear

Fear is an aspect of the primitive urge of self-preservation. It is the source of many emotions. We usually do not realize the multitude of fears which we have and the degree to which they affect us. Many of us go through each day consciously or unconsciously preoccupied with a variety of fears. Fear is one of the main sources of our motivation. It is a fountainhead of emotions which must be rechanneled if we are to live in happiness and joy.

If our existence, our sense of self-worth or completeness depends upon our having something from outside and we anticipate the loss of that object or the inability to gain what we need, we then experience fear. For example, we might fear walking down a dark street or going into an unlighted basement because of a sense that our very life may be threatened. If we feel insecure and incomplete without approval from others, we may approach each interaction with a fear of being rejected.

Without a habit of dependency there could be no fear. We would allow objects and experiences to come and go without trying to cling to them. But when we feel the intense dependency on something we are inevitably afraid of losing it. A farmer may fear that his crops will perish in a cold spell, a child may fear the loss of her mother, an investor the loss in value of his stocks. Whatever we feel that we must have and whatever we have incorporated into our identities is what we fear losing.

Unfortunately, being fearful that something will happen has the quality of a self-fulfilling prophecy. That is, the things that we fear sometimes come true, but only because we fear them in the first place. For example, if you fear rejection from others your lack of ease may be expressed in your speech and non-verbal communications, through mannerisms and gestures. The negative manner in which you approach relationships will be picked up by the person to whom you are relating, and returned to you. If you are fearful and hold back, anticipating rejection, the other person will respond to your holding back with reticence of his own. This in turn will be interpreted by you as the rejection you anticipated and so you may withdraw even more. In this way a vicious circle is created. The more we approach any situation with doubt and fear, the more likely it is that the very thing we fear will come about. In a similar way, fear of attack may actually cause the attack we fear. An animal may leave one person unharmed but attack another who is fearful of it, for an animal will usually sense that person's fear. It senses that if we are frightened we are likely to attack, and so it attacks first. Thus fear invites danger. By merely eliminating the fear we may also prevent that negative experience from occurring.

In many situations in our lives we may find that we bring upon ourselves the very things of which we are afraid. There may even be some value in this, for it leads us to face what we fear and in so doing we often come to realize that the situation is not as fearful as it seemed. Our imagination tends to distort the picture, and we can save ourselves from a good deal of pain if we realize this.

Yoga psychology explains that the fears which we have can be eliminated through learning to examine them with an impartial attitude, uncovering those underlying addictions and dependencies which make us afraid. As we gain confidence in ourselves our fears will dissolve. Furthermore, as we look at our fears in an objective way, we will come to realize that the vast majority of the things that we fear never come to pass. Most of our chronic fears are irrational. They are based on false and negative imaginings. But only a small percentage of these events actually come to pass. Thus we spend considerable time worrying and thinking about the future rather than fully experiencing and enjoying the present. Our fears are unproductive and they incapacitate us in dealing with our present situation.

Living with fears means living in the world of imagination with fancy and fantasy. Rather than squarely facing the fact that everything in life is subject to change, we desperately try to hold on to objects and situations. With such an attitude, fear is inevitable. But sooner or later we will have to let go of that which we claim as ours. Our new car will eventually rust and break down. Our children will grow and strike out on their own. Clinging to the things to which we are attached is like fighting our way upstream, struggling against the basic law of change which pervades our universe. And this struggle can only bring us pain and unhappiness.

But it is possible to avoid this state of mind and to live in harmony with ourselves. As our consciousness grows, we gradually learn to see our external universe in a new way. Instead of looking for something outside of ourselves and then fearing its loss, we learn to relate to people and objects with less dependency. We come to appreciate the beauty and the joy which they give without grasping and seeking to make that joy permanent beyond its time.

The only person who is free from fear is he who has gradually gained freedom from his false imaginings. Such a person will realize that he cannot depend on the external world for abiding joy and happiness. Those things which temporarily give us pleasure will not stay with us forever. But that which is part of our very nature, part of our very being, cannot leave us. When we direct our attention inward, when we look there for our joy and satisfaction, we find a sense of fulfillment which always abides with us, for it is no different from us. We will achieve freedom from fear when we realize that the source of fulfillment is within rather than in that external world of objects and events.

When we reach this understanding we will have a new freedom in relating to the external world. We can then accept and enjoy what comes our way. We can see that the objects of this world are here for our use, for our experience, for our happiness. The people with whom we relate are here to share our joy. But we need not have a clinging attitude in our relationships. We can let go if the time is ripe, just as the tree lets go of its fruit.

Whenever we cling to something, we experience a constriction which brings pain and misery. This is evident even through a simple exercise of tightening and tensing our muscles. When we let go of that tension, we relax and come to feel much better. Tension is always a process of constriction, physical or mental. Being tense and fearful is a sign that something is wrong in our emotional life, just as physical pain is a sign of a physical problem. Tensions and fears indicate that we are clinging to somebody or something too tightly. Such pain can only be relieved by psychologically letting go, giving up our possessive attitude.

When we have learned to let go, we will have found one of the greatest secrets in all of life for experiencing peace and happiness. Letting go is always accompanied by a feeling of opening, blossoming and coming into a new and more encompassing space. We fear letting go of our dependency on objects and people, but if we are truly able to do so we will find that what is gained is greater than that which is left behind. At whatever level letting go takes place, it brings a rich harvest of unexpected rewards.

Greed

Greed is an emotion which inspires one to have something more and more. There is no end to this emotion. It does not know how to say no. A greedy man becomes self-conceited and remains always insecure and troubled. No matter how much he holds and accumulates, he is not likely to feel that he has enough, because a calamity can always be imagined in which everything will be lost. His greed prevents him from communicating, growing and loving others. Unfortunately psychology today does not give the right solution to greed and other harmful emotions which rob us of our peace of mind.

Greed arises out of fear; this fear can never be overcome by hoarding material possessions. We can never get to a point where we feel secure if we start with a basic premise of insecurity. The only way that the unpleasant psychological state that accompanies greed can be overcome is through finding security within ourselves, and realizing that it is not dependent on externals. As long as we rely on externals we are subject to this emotion, and we will never feel that we have enough. We often find that the person who is most happy is the one who has the least, for such a person starts with the sense of fullness and shares it with others rather than looking for what he can find to fill himself up.

This does not mean that it is necessary to abandon our possessions to find happiness, but merely to abandon our attitude of clinging and dependence upon things. If we understand that all the things that we have are meant to help us in attaining our aim of life and that we should not establish proprietorship by being greedy, then our main problem will be over. We can have all the things that we need without becoming concerned and preoccupied with ownership.

The cultivation of charity is one of the best means of overcoming greed. Charity is considered to be one of the greatest virtues; however, a great deal of what is done in the name of charity is not genuine. There are three

approaches which people take in giving charity. These
are explained in all the great religious psychologies of the
world. Some people do charity to satisfy their egos and to
feel important; others do charity because they believe
good will come to them as a result of their good deeds.
These two approaches toward giving charity do little to
overcome greed because they are based upon what the
giver will himself receive. But the wise do charity without
seeking anything in return and thus get freedom from this
violent emotion.

Depression

Continued failures in attaining one's goal diminish
one's inspiration and finally leads to disappointment and
depression. One feels he is not fit or successful and
becomes absorbed in self-condemnation. The motivation
for action is diminished and one remains captive within
one's own world of thoughts and desires. The depressive
person is no longer turned outward toward the world, but
is absorbed in giving himself attention. He is nursing and
nurturing that injured part of himself, by being introverted
and living inside the boundaries built by his
petty-mindedness.

This state of mind can also be brought on by the loss
of what has already been attained, or by a separation from
another person. Here there is a feeling that a part of us is
missing, that we are no longer whole. Sometimes we
seek to escape such depression by simply replacing the lost
object with another. We may think, "I'll feel better if I
buy a new dress or a new car." But this substitution does

not release depression. At best it merely postpones the underlying feeling of incompleteness. Sometimes it can even strengthen it, for at some level we realize that the new object is not really what we need to feel whole.* Substitution, replacement or sublimation does not finally help such a person. Gradual systematic training, using reason in observing various levels of our personality and the underlying causes of such emotions, is more helpful. This may be called the way of self-training.

Some people learn to be discontented no matter how much they possess, for they do not appreciate and admire their own way of living, thinking and understanding. In such cases, being deprived of a loved object is not the cause of depression, but being depressed becomes part of one's nature. Such people find no joy within or without. No one can please them and nothing seems to help them. Is there any solution for such depressed people? Yes, there is. If they are made aware that their whole character and personality are molded by their deep-rooted habits, then perhaps new grooves can be made for the mind to travel along. New habits can be formed and strengthened, but it takes some effort and training. Sometimes such training needs physical, mental and spiritual discipline and a well organized program of therapy. Yoga psychology offers such an education combining a few gentle exercises with breathing methods, meditation and methods of self-study.

Many people undergoing psychotherapy talk about

---

* This is why many people feel an unexpected sense of depression upon receiving a gift.

feeling hollow inside. They try to fill up this emptiness through eating, through going to parties, through accumulating many possessions and "friends." But such patients report that the emptiness remains, that whatever they acquire is merely superficial and cannot take away their basic problem. They may, in fact, feel that in spite of all their activities life itself is empty. One young man reported to us that when he was younger he would walk about downtown in the different cities in which he had been, looking for someone or something that would make him feel complete, perhaps the young girl walking toward him, or the sports car in a store window, or the music and "merriment" on the other side of the tavern door. But in all of his searching he was disappointed. He never found anything that was fulfilling to him. He never found a person who was not looking back at him in that same search.

Finally, he met his spiritual teacher, and he knew that he was home at last. He realized that in all of his experiences he was actually looking for a guide to help him journey from these emotional problems to enlightenment. His spiritual teacher helped him to see that the real cause of his depression was his lack of enlightenment. He came to know this root cause of all emotional depressions and then started searching in the right direction.

When we come to know the changing temperaments of our thought patterns, likes and dislikes, then we find the value of objects increasing and decreasing. It all depends on our taste, interest, desire and habits. As long as we remain within the boundaries of sense objects and selfish motivations, we do not become aware of that center of fullness within ourselves. By studying the lives of great people, by practicing meditation, by going through therapy, we become aware of something higher and, sometimes, the center of consciousness within.

No object can quench the thirst for enlightenment. Some individuals remain depressed for this reason. They find that all the objects and experiences they encounter do not have the capacity to provide lasting fulfillment. How many of us have walked the streets searching, finding a glimmer here and there, only to be disappointed sooner or later and begin our search again. There is a yogic saying, "Painted cakes do not satisfy hunger." How many are the painted cakes that we have found.

For help in this situation the therapy of enlightenment is the highest one. It has been used since ages ago and is being used even today while we are beating around the bush. Exactly as a room which was dark for a hundred years is illuminated in a second's time when the light is switched on, so the emotional life and personality of the seeker is immediately transformed when he experiences this enlightenment. We human beings without awareness of the higher reality identify ourselves with our emotions and desires. The day we become aware of the reality, we will know the values of all the objects as they are, and there will be no reason for depression.

Pride

Pride is an emotion which can be as intense as the other emotions which have been described. It can be either a beneficial or a harmful emotion. The pride that builds self-confidence and inner growth is helpful but the pride that prevents one from learning is dangerous as are other negative emotions.

The development of pride forms a step in the ladder of growth from a sense of weakness, incompetence and dependency on others to the development of self-confidence and assertiveness. It helps create a degree of self-sufficiency in growing children and in those who feel insecure. This is why we often encourage children and others who are uncertain of themselves to develop pride.

However, there comes a point in the course of development where pride stands in the way of further growth. At one point it helped to lift us to a more capable level of accomplishment, but later, as we seek to elevate ourselves further, pride becomes an anchor which weighs us down. For when pride increases sufficiently, self-confidence is replaced by self-preoccupation. Pride then accentuates our differentiation from others. It closes us off from true relationships. Someone who has developed pride to a great degree is likely not to listen to others or take others into account. He will be reluctant to admit his mistakes lest his feeling of pride be weakened. Such exaggerated pride or "false pride" is often an outer show which covers a continuing underlying sense of inadequacy. The person who is truly confident in himself will not be so self-absorbed and narrow, but will feel more comfortable in exposing his errors and weaknesses and in giving credit to and humbling himself before others.

Pride also keeps us out of touch with our deeper center of integration. It is based on the false idea that the ego is the center of our being and is really in control. The feeling of pride involves a misappropriation, giving credit for our accomplishments to the ego rather than to that deeper center of intuitive wisdom within. If we are to continue in the evolution of our consciousness it is necessary to transcend the narrow preoccupations of pride and to develop an awareness of something more encompassing than our own egos.

Finally we will come to surrender our self-preoccupation and become aware of a deeper level of guidance, the Self. As we become more aware of this center, we will begin to do our work as an expression of the integrating forces coming from the Self rather than acting for the enhancement of the ego. When we transcend preoccupation with ourselves merely as individuals, our conflicts, miseries and wars will be left behind, and we will experience the harmony and joy of union. We will find a new security, realizing our place in the grand design. Even a very partial awareness of the Self can become a greater source of inspiration than personal pride. Surprisingly as we give up the pride that once helped us to be more productive, we actually become more effective in our work, because we are acting with greater harmony.

The Western spiritual traditions help individuals to transcend egocentricity by fostering the attitude that "There is something greater than I; I'm not so all-important." In this teaching the deeper center of consciousness is externalized in its conceptualization, and prayer is used as a way of bringing out a sense of humility and an attitude of selfless service. For example, the Lord's Prayer says: " . . . hallowed be Thy name. *Thy* kingdom come, *Thy* will be done . . . ." The focus of this and other prayers is on the glorification of higher consciousness and a humbling of oneself in relationship to it. Such prayers enable us to transcend pride by teaching us to trust that spiritual source which extends beyond the ego level of awareness. As our ego is humbled, we experience the sense of peace and harmony that comes from this higher level of awareness.

Methods for Transforming Unpleasant Emotions

Emotion is stronger than thought power. When a violent emotion arises, it disturbs the entire thinking process. After attaining emotional maturity, however, thoughts can be guided properly. All control is emotional. All the great works were done at the height of emotional maturity. Both Eastern and Western psychologies are aware of the fact that emotion is a great power if it is properly channeled and also is very dangerous if it is not understood by human beings.

According to Eastern psychology, there are several therapeutic methods available for evoking higher consciousness and thereby transforming the lower emotions. One means is channeling the emotions through devotional methods such as chanting, singing hymns, and studying the scriptures. Patanjali, the codifier of yoga science, says that remembering a mantra with *bhava*, or one-pointed devotion, is very important. Remembering the mantra on the thought level is easily disturbed by the emotions, but once the mantra is assimilated by the feelings, control is attained. If *bhava* or the devotional emotion is cultivated, *bhava samadhi* (devotional ecstasy) is achieved in no time. Those who follow the path of *Bhakti Yoga*, the yoga of devotion, are aware that all the emotions can be channeled and directed toward the center of consciousness.

Another method is to use the intellect and rationality to understand the various aspects of life within and without. The faculty of discrimination is used to attain the Void spoken of in Buddhism. A similar method is used by the Vedantins to attain the Absolute Reality. It makes the aspirant aware that Absolute Reality is not anything different from his own inner Self. Instead of identifying himself with the objects, the student learns to identify himself with the Reality. Prayer is not considered to be one of the methods of attaining the higher Reality. Prayer has definite and positive results, but the realization of the higher nature of man strengthens and makes him aware of the reality, "Thou art That."

Another method is the systematic study of all levels of life: the environment, the body, the breath, the mind and its different functions, the individual soul and its oneness with the Absolute Reality. There is still another method where one offers the fruits of his actions, selflessly, with full devotion to the Lord. In this path work is worship. One becomes aware that he is an instrument of a higher integrating quality. He seeks to make himself as perfect an instrument as possible. There are also several other subtler and finer methods which are equally authentic and helpful in purifying, polishing and preparing the internal states. They help one to gain inner strength and become a good human being, free from emotional problems.

THE POSITIVE EMOTIONS

The Evolution of Desire

Emotional immaturity exists when we are tossed by many desires for the objects of the world. Our relationship with these objects is always in flux. As we gain and lose that which we desire we are bound to experience the various negative emotions as long as we have strong desires for these objects. Fortunately there is a way out of this predicament. For in addition to the desires that grow out of the primitive urges, there is another type of desire. This is the desire for higher knowledge which helps in maintaining the flame of love for learning. It is entirely different from the desires which lead toward the unpleasant emotions. Higher knowledge is that knowledge which helps human beings in channeling all the primitive urges and the springs of emotions.

When a desire for higher knowledge dawns and the necessity for that higher knowledge is strongly felt, one becomes more and more one-pointed. Finally all other desires are swallowed by that one desire as all the waves are swallowed by a big wave of the ocean. When we have awakened to that higher knowledge, we give up our dependency on the world of objects where change and decay are predominant, and transfer our search to that which abides. Once that higher knowledge is attained, the grief and woe that come from worldly desires are transcended. People go on receiving things of the world yet they are never satisfied. But if their desire for attaining reality and truth is fulfilled, they can live with fewer objects of the world. Then life becomes meaningful, purposeful.

In addition to negative desires, positive desires and one-pointed desire that have been described, there is a fourth desire. This is a desire for the welfare of others. This fourth desire makes one selfless. One lives in the world not for his selfish ends, but for doing selfless actions for others. Such a desire does not bind, but becomes a means of liberation.

In the *Katha Upanishad*, Nachiketa, a selfless and pure aspirant, was given three boons by Yama, the Lord of Death. But he did not ask to receive anything for himself; he asked for others. As his third boon he desired wisdom concerning life and death. Yama tried to tempt him. First he offered him worldly pleasures, then celestial pleasures, but Natchiketa was not tempted; he had no such desires. Finally Yama had to reveal the secrets of life here and hereafter and then Natchiketa was satisfied.

Love

Among all the positive emotions, love is the finest. It can be known, understood and verified through our mind, action and speech. It is one emotion that has given hope to humanity, but it is obviously misunderstood. Love is the source of life and a wonderful expression in its fullest expansion. All of the great works in the world were done by the great lovers of humanity. Without love there is no possibility of any success in the world or in spiritual attainment. This positive emotion is the biggest gift to human beings. It is often said that even death has no power to change human destiny. If anything at all has that power, it is love.

But when we study life we find that the child loves his parents for himself, because his needs are fulfilled by the parents. That type of love is different from love as it is being described here. In life we find two principles; one is expansion and another is contraction. If one learns to expand one's consciousness by selfless action, speech and thoughts, he can attain the highest rank in human life. But if he becomes selfish, he can contract his vision, thinking, and entire living by leading a miserable life. Actually a selfish man corrupts and misuses the word "love."

Love is a creative way of living and being. It is a simple path, that can be taken by anyone, anywhere. The path to enlightenment becomes easy if this emotion is used rightly. But love in day-to-day life is often misused in wanting fulfillment of a desire. Selfish love or love for a human being is entirely different from love of God or Divinity. When a human being soars high and reaches the fountainhead of life and light, love flows spontaneously through him and is really helpful to humanity. Even in the world when one does something selflessly without any return, for the service of humanity, that subtlest action is motivated by love. Otherwise the love we use in the world creates attachment, and attachment brings bondage, misery and ignorance. Love alone gives freedom.

Joy

Joy is the first-born of love and is experienced by all creatures. A human being can experience joy through thoughts, action and speech which soothes his senses and stimulates his nervous system. Joy is a necessity in human life. It repairs the physical and mental damage brought on by one's way of day-to-day living.

Life without joy is a light that shines only for the dead. A fortunate few know how to utilize this joyous state of mind. Joy is very necessary for maintaining harmony within oneself and in one's relationships in the world, at home and in society.

Peace

A joyous mind spontaneously flows toward a state of tranquility where the different qualities of the mind* get together and attain a state of harmony. Such harmonious life is essential for longevity. When the understanding grows, one starts realizing that peace of mind and harmony are most essential for all human beings.

A peaceful mind is never disturbed by the charms and attractions of the world, but always helps the aspirant in attaining the wisdom he needs. Peace of mind does not make anyone negative or passive. One who has attained peace and harmony attains a state of equilibrium

---

* In yogic psychology, identified as *sattva, rajas* and *tamas*.

and such an orderly mind alone is an instrument to fathom the deeper levels of life. All of the spiritual practices lead the aspirant to attain that state of which the *Katha Upanishad*, the *Bhagavad Gita* and other great scriptures of the world sing praises, that state of equanimity which is attainable by having this positive emotion called peace.

A peaceful, loving man is a God-loving man who has established himself in his essential nature called *sat-chit-ananda*, or existence, knowledge and bliss. If such a man lives in the world, he is undisturbed by the worldly fetters. He is called *jiva mukta*, liberated here and now.

8

Love and Forgiveness

The quality of mercy . . . is twice bless'd: It blesseth him that gives and him that takes.

Shakespeare

Among all the creatures in the world the human being is the finest and among all human beings, the finest is he who knows that the lord of life is love. One who knows how to give love is truly a server of humanity. Forgiveness is a virtue which is essential in developing love. These two qualities, love and forgiveness, increase with the growth of humanity. When a human being starts thinking about the purpose of life and studies its various aspects he eventually understands the value of these two qualities.

Humanity has been experimenting by using these resources for the great leaders in the past found out that these qualities equip a human being with divine attributes. Without love and forgiveness one cannot attain divinity. Love means giving selflessly; forgiveness means going forward and not brooding on the past. All human beings have to face the problems of false egotism, pride, selfishness and petty-mindedness. As long as one remains within the bounds of these negative attributes one cannot expand himself to his highest being. Gradually these can be replaced with forgiveness and love which are very essential in our day to day life. The great people of various nations of the world have some similarity and universality in their outlook on life; these two qualities are predominant in their lives, actually these two qualities make them the architects of human civilization. But most of us have not come to terms with our condemnation of ourselves and others. We have not learned how to use our mental and emotional resources properly.

There is a faculty of judging in every human being in varying degrees. Some people cultivate and sharpen this faculty and then they decide things properly. Some use this faculty to judge the actions of others, but they do not apply the same criteria in judging their own actions and improving their own behavior. All too often we spontaneously judge the behavior of others without understanding the motivation behind their behavior and that is why our judgment is often wrong. This is one of the biggest barriers that we find in communication today. If we apply the law, "do unto others as you do to yourself," perhaps we will commit fewer mistakes in judging others. Insightful self-judgment is a rare attribute. We typically judge others and judge ourselves superficially without appreciating the basic potentials and qualities which we have.

Seeking Justice

Often, without realizing it, we spend a great deal of our time and energy condemning ourselves and others. We put other people into categories of good and bad according to their actions. If we see someone behaving in a way we do not consider right, we become critical. We may speak against him or merely think of him in a negative way. We also judge our own behavior according to our own convenience, approving of some things and disapproving of others. If we do not live up to our own expectations or if we commit a blunder, we might think to ourselves, "I'm so incompetent, I'm really stupid." We carry these judgmental notions with us almost all the time. Such thoughts repeatedly run through our minds, focusing on the inadequacies in ourselves and others.

One part of ourselves has taken on this role of a judge. This judge sits in his own chamber within the maze of our mind. His manner is stern and harsh as he calls us to order and asks us to account for ourselves. He takes no excuses and ignores pleading. Whatever information comes before him is strictly evaluated. At times he may smile with approval but more often darkness engulfs his countenance as he becomes dissatisfied and disapproving. As long as we feel that we have the right to condemn or to approve, to pass sentence on ourselves and others, we give the judge a powerful position within the government of our mind.

There are individual differences in the degree to which we engage in judgmental behavior. This is related to how much insecurity one feels. Psychologists who have studied people with a predominance of this trait in their personalities have often described them as authoritarian and compulsive. There is a vast literature in modern psychology describing such personality types. Certain professions such as law or accounting, where keeping the record straight is important, are often sought out by such judgmental personalities and provide very suitable roles for them. These roles allow them to function well in the world. Compulsive traits such as overly frequent hand washing, being neat and clean to the extreme, always doing what one is told by those in authority and seeking control over others who have less status are characteristics of the judgmental person. Such people typically do not experience much joy in their lives. Their faces are often drawn and may express distaste, or a businesslike attitude toward life.

But it is not always the person on the right side of the law who is preoccupied with good and bad. Those who commit crimes are equally concerned with justice. They represent the other side of the same duality. In fact the two—the judge (or law enforcer) and the criminal—create and sustain one another in their common concern over right and wrong.

When we lead psychotherapy groups in prisons we are surprised at how much the prisoners are concerned with justice. The majority of them feel that they have been grossly mistreated. Many assert that the courts have "railroaded" them, that they have not been given a fair trial. Others argue that they have been abused by the prison officers, the institution, and society throughout their prison term. In fact, most prisoners seem to be preoccupied with judging others. Judging and being judged seem to occur together. As one is judged so he judges and as one judges so is he judged.

In the prison setting both the officer and the prisoner feel that they are in the right. The prisoner seeks to get even for abuses from the officer and the officer wants to give the prisoner "what's coming to him" for his sullen, negative behavior. Each is equally concerned with balancing the scales of justice as he sees it, and in so doing they are at war with one another. For each has a different point of view in looking at the situation.

And so it is whenever we try to seek justice and to determine what is good and what is bad. The limited vision and perspective of each individual upsets the balance of the scale, for all too often we imagine that the other has an advantage and so add more weight on our side. We complain again and again that we have not been treated fairly by the law, by others, or by society. We have not gotten what is due to us. After all, didn't we work hard? Didn't we do the right thing? And look what we have gotten back to show for it!

We do not realize that in demanding equality we are actually creating the injustice that comes back to us. We are disrespectful and abusive to others in our demands, and we inevitably create a reaction which often brings us more harsh treatment than before. And it turns out that in this struggle to gain an advantage over the other in the name of justice no advantage is actually gained by anyone. Both sides lose in the atmosphere of hostility and revenge that is generated.

We have thus far talked in the extreme, describing the compulsively righteous person and the rebellious criminal.

But each of us harbors these two characters within us. From time to time and in different degrees we assume the role of the upright judge and policeman and then of the rebellious child or adolescent who "will set things right when he gets the upper hand." Learning how to deal with and neutralize these attitudes within ourselves would be of great help in eliminating the pain that they cause.

Many things happen throughout our life that from our perspective may seem unfair, as if we really did not deserve them. When this occurs we can take either of two attitudes. We can seek retribution, engaging in what we think is justified anger, hostility and vengeance, giving ourselves an excuse to be abusive and destructive toward others. If we follow this course we will create for ourselves a life of unhappiness and misery. But another alternative is open to us, when we take exactly the opposite attitude, when we say, "OK, perhaps I've felt mistreated and abused, but instead of seeking what's due me I'll forgive and forget."

Forgiving Others

"I forgive you." These three words are so powerful that they can suddenly change the darkness that we experience about us into the pure light of a new day. As soon as you experience forgiveness your whole demeanor, your attitude and your personality change dramatically. Instead of being tormented by the hate and vengeful feelings that are carried inside in seeking justice, you experience a warm expansiveness. As you let go of those negative feelings, and of the rationalizations that gave you the excuse to get even you find yourself beginning to experience a common bond you share with others. The sense of rigidity and of being shut off within yourself is replaced by a feeling of comfort. All this is achieved by simply saying, "It's no big thing. I don't have to get even. I'll just let go."

When you practice forgiveness and love you find that others begin to treat you differently. Instead of reacting to your revengeful attitude with their own closed-off distrust, other people begin to open up and share their warmth with you. As they become aware of your forgiving attitude, they realize that they no longer have to fear your judgment and wrath. They can be themselves and be comfortable with you. Others will appreciate this to such a degree that they will open themselves to you and give whatever they can.

So, in forgiving others, we become the recipients of comfort, peace and happiness. It turns out that the way we treat others creates a situation that leads us to be treated in the same way. When we forgive others we soon find that they begin to hold less against us. We need not be so fearful of their harsh judgments. This law of human existence was clearly expressed long ago in the Lord's Prayer: "Forgive us our trespasses as we forgive those who trespass against us." Many people look at this statement as merely a request, asking the Lord, who is seen as separate from them, that they be forgiven the way they forgive others. But no request need be made, for there is an exact and inevitable correspondence: to the extent that we forgive others we are forgiven, and the very act of forgiving is in itself a forgiveness of ourselves.

This is the law of forgiveness.

There is an exact correspondence between our experience of forgiving and the experience of being forgiven. We can only open ourselves up to the experience of the other's forgiveness to the extent that we ourselves have developed a forgiving attitude. For we are being forgiven always but we do not know it when we are preoccupied with judging ourselves and others.

It is not necessary to take our word that such a law exists. You can test it for yourself. Merely become aware of where and when you feel judgmental and critical of others, or feel that you have been abused and wish to get back. Then just sit quietly and think for some minutes of forgiveness until you genuinely feel yourself forgiving the other, letting go of your judgment or criticism. See for yourself how your attitude changes and what psychological effect is produced. Have you lost something or have you gained? Become aware when a critical, condemning attitude arises within you and each time work with yourself in this way. Try it for only a week and notice the reactions of others. See how relationships change. You might say, "How can I forgive people who have abused and mistreated me?" But if we could see more deeply into our relationships we would realize that we bring these experiences on through our own actions, we would see that there is nobody to be forgiven. The people who mistreat us are often acting out the part that we assign to them.

There is a line in a prayer by St. Francis: "It is in pardoning that we are pardoned." In the act of pardoning we think we are doing something wonderful for the person we are forgiving, but actually we are doing something much more wonderful for ourselves. For that very act creates for us an entirely different frame of reference. Because love and forgiveness allow us to experience the world in such a harmonious way it turns out that we are really pardoning ourselves. We are throwing off all the hate and the vengeance that we ordinarily harbor and acquiring a new sense of inner freedom. What could be more perfect justice than that?

Some people might feel that in forgiving others they are opening themselves to being taken advantage of. They might say, "If I keep forgiving everyone they'll get away with all kinds of things." This is a misconception. In fact condemnation often does not prevent behavior but fans the flames so that the unwanted behavior increases. If the other person sees that it gets you upset he may do the same thing again for that very reason.

Forgiving does not mean allowing people to walk all over you and abuse you. Nor does it mean that you should not try to prevent others from overstepping their bounds, from being callous and inconsiderate. Setting limits for another person is often helpful to him, whereas letting that person take advantage of you merely teaches him that he can hurt and injure others without concern. This does not give him a chance to develop respect and care for the other. The person who allows others to take advantage of him is not practicing forgiveness but is actually attempting to repress his hostile and aggressive feelings, hiding them beneath external acquiescence and acceptance. Often we see this quality amongst those who have been following a set of religious precepts. In trying to practice forgiveness they mistakenly decide that they should allow themselves to be used by others. While they outwardly appear to be pleasant and forgiving, there may be smoldering resentment beneath the surface. There is a vast difference between outward acquiescence which masks resentment and a genuine inner sense of forgiveness.

Let us now look at a typical example of what happens when we confuse the outward appearance of forgiveness with the real thing: A person you have known for some time comes to visit your home and behaves rudely with you. From time to time he tells you about faults he sees in you. He takes food from the refrigerator and when he is finished eating leaves the containers out on the counter along with the dirty dishes. He stays up late at night with the TV playing loudly while you try to sleep. While you resent your guest's behavior and wish he would leave, you do not say anything to him. You have created an image in which you believe yourself to be a good, kind, and considerate person, someone who would not hurt anyone's feelings. So you keep your resentment inside, secretly thinking of things that might happen to him that would "teach him a lesson" or would even the score for the way he abused you. But outwardly you remain pleasant and cordial, cleaning up the mess he has made and sleeping with a pillow over your head.

You may think that you are practicing forgiveness, but your outward behavior does not reflect your true feelings. While you pretend that you are acting in a forgiving manner, a closer examination may actually reveal subtle critical remarks and hostile thoughts. This situation may lead to any of a number of consequences. For example, you may develop physical symptoms as a result of the pressure of unreleased emotions. Or perhaps you will continue to collect a list of all the things your visitor has done wrong until you feel "righteous and justified" in telling him how he has abused you. Then you feel the walled-in anger filling you and bursting out in a tirade as you tell him of all the inconsiderate acts he has committed. It feels good to be releasing these feelings at last.

In this characterization forgiveness was understood as an attitude which expressed itself in outward acquiescence. But actually forgiveness is an inner attitude which is not necessarily revealed by outwardly giving in to someone. All too often in many areas of our lives we try to cheat ourselves and others by substituting an outer appearance for the real thing. We mimic genuine forgiveness until sooner or later our true sentiments are revealed beneath the facade.

Real forgiveness involves releasing all condemnation and genuinely valuing the other person. Outwardly you may still find it necessary to be firm and to set clear limits on another. But this firmness can be expressed from an inner and interpersonal harmony rather than a sense of justified annoyance or criticism.

Forgiving Yourself

The extend to which we genuinely forgive others is very closely related to the extent to which we give up self-condemnation. We might even say that there are two aspects of the same experience. This truth is often expressed in our common-sense psychology. How often have you heard it said that what we dislike about others are the very things that we do not like about ourselves, that those people whom we dislike often have the same traits as we do. If we have tendencies that we would rather not admit within ourselves but see them manifested in others, we often approach those people with antagonism. Think about those for whom you have developed a strong dislike, and ask yourself whether they may not be reflecting something you disapprove of in your own person.

All too often we are highly critical and demeaning of ourselves. We may mask such negative feelings with an outward veneer of self-approval and self-interest, but beneath this surface assurance, the judge is carrying on his work. People set rigid standards of conduct for themselves and, as a result, often find that they do not live up to their expectations. Then the judge within them pronounces a "guilty" verdict and sentences them to feel that guilt. Those who have tried to live up to an exacting religious code or to rigid moral norms which they may have learned as young children, often experience intense guilt feelings. People may feel guilty about all sorts of behavior which does not meet the particular criteria they have for themselves. For some the expression of anger may lead to guilt, for others it is a sexual desire.

It is frequently the case that those who become involved in yoga bring with them their overly-judgmental attitudes and set stern standards for themselves. They establish ideals for their behavior which they have not prepared themselves to follow. So, for example, a student may decide to meditate a given amount of hours per day, to get up before sunrise, and to completely change his eating habits. Rather than gradually developing the ability to achieve these goals he wants to do it all at once. He then feels considerable guilt after he has turned off the alarm clock for several days in a row to go back to sleep for two more hours, or has interrupted his new diet by indulging in a large piece of chocolate cake. It is not unusual for yoga students to become absorbed in and dejected over their lack of discipline and self-control. Rather than working in a slow stepwise fashion, they immediately chastize themselves for their first failures, bringing forth their old pattern of self condemnation.

A skilled teacher will use such reactions as an opportunity for the aspirant to learn something about himself. The teacher will direct him to observe this pattern of setting too high a standard and then feeling guilty for falling short of it. He may guide the student to study his guilt feelings and to see whether they serve a useful purpose in helping him grow and develop or whether they lead him to become self-absorbed and negativistic. The student may find that such feelings lead him to avoid responsibility. As long as he feels that he is inadequate and a failure, he need no longer put forth the effort toward slow progress. The purpose and goal of yoga is to help one evaluate and cope more realistically with oneself and with the experiences that one faces. Yoga psychology teaches the aspirant to handle those unreasonable expectations and fantasies that he has created for himself. The yoga student learns, rather than to blame himself, to readjust his expectations and to make them more realistic in terms of what he can really achieve.

We often find that those who create the most idealized expectations for themselves are the least able to sustain their commitment to a discipline. Students who are initially extremely enthusiastic about following a path such as yoga are often the first to become disillusioned and turn away in search of a new fantasized ideal. The well-known fable about the hare and the tortoise shows itself clearly to the teacher of yoga who finds again and again that the slow but steadily progressing aspirant whose expectations for himself are modest makes the greatest progress in the end.

In learning to be more realistic about himself and the world, the aspirant is encouraged to set goals which he can reach and not to take his lack of instant achievement as worthy of reprimand. He must learn to forgive himself, to let go of all those feelings of guilt and inadequacy. For out of such negative attitudes toward oneself, out of such stern and harsh self-condemnation there cannot grow a sense of joy, peace and harmony. If one is to find peace and joy, destructive self-criticism must be left behind and replaced with the attitude of compassion for oneself.

The replacement of harshness toward yourself with forgiveness is not so difficult to achieve. Just note those times when you find yourself being critical, when you condemn yourself and see yourself in a bad light. Try as frequently as you can to be aware of those moments when the judge is active and exerting his influence. Then begin to introduce a new quality which will expand his range of choices. Teach the judge that he can pardon as well as condemn. Allow the judge to forgive whatever it may be you feel that you have done wrong. You may find that the judge comes to enjoy this new function. His old habits of harsh condemnation may reappear, but if you can watch this happening and simply allow feelings of forgiveness to wash over you each time criticism occurs, you will eventually find a new habit where the old had been.

Each time you begin to blame and downgrade yourself, simply think of forgiveness and feel that forgiveness permeate your whole being. Feel it again and again until it overrides any thoughts of self-criticism. Put notes saying "Forgive Yourself" in your pockets. Put this message on the wall until it is so much a part of you that you do not need these any more. If you have hurt someone, if you have done something destructive, forgive yourself and allow that sentiment to be expressed throughout your being. This does not mean that you should condone the behavior and feel free to commit the act again, but by forgiving yourself you will allow that act to be left behind. Rather than be absorbed in it, brood over it and draw out its consequences, just dismiss it from your mind and let yourself begin afresh.

For example, if you are with your children and your goal is not to get angry but you fail at this, instead of brooding about what a bad parent you are, you can say to yourself, "That's not really what I want to do. I want to learn how not to get upset with the children. I didn't do it today, but instead of worrying about it and being hateful toward myself I'll forgive myself and try again.

Instead of getting caught up in all the things I did wrong in the past and making myself feel miserable about it, I'll just focus on what I'm doing now and do that as perfectly as I can."

Judging yourself is holding on, perpetuating an inner conflict. It is living in the past and bringing that past into the present. But forgiving is letting go. It is an act of relaxing, of opening up and coming into the new moment, using this opportunity to start again and to behave in a way that will bring joy and accord. Judging and holding on are the experience of stagnation, tightness and suffering, but forgiving is the very process of rejuvenation and growth. Living in the light of love and forgiveness will give you peace and you will really experience that sunshine that radiates within and all around you. Many of those things that you do not like about yourself will drop away as you create a positive accepting attitude. And eventually the forgiveness which you express toward yourself will begin to emanate from your being and to be felt and enjoyed by others.

Some people make the mistake of thinking that feelings of guilt and self-criticism are noble because they indicate humility and lack of egotism. But, in fact, this is a mere mimicry of humility, for being absorbed in self-condemnation is merely a form of self-indulgence. One constantly dwells on the "I," experiencing an unadmittedly pleasurable state, a mixed pleasure derived from pain, which is described in common parlance as "liking to suffer." So guilt is really a self-preoccupation, whereas forgiveness is a harmonious experience reaching both inward and outward. It involves a turning toward the experience of the Self, the deeper essence of our being and a reaching out toward others with love and acceptance.

The quality of forgiveness is the very essence of a spiritual leader. If you have the rare and fortunate opportunity to be with a true master you will eventually become aware that forgiveness and unconditional love are his chief qualities. Many people have a great fear of coming face to face with such a master because they feel that all of their deficiencies and inadequacies will be unmasked. They may believe that the master is completely aware of and sees all of their faults, dishonesty, greed and anger. So instead of coming face to face, they turn themselves away. If they would but look, though, they would see in his eyes no harsh criticism, no condemnation, merely acceptance, whatever their thoughts, words and deeds might have been. The master sees it all and yet understands the perfect harmony of it all, and thus he accepts all aspects of your being. In understanding the perfection of your each and every act, he is beyond forgiving; his abode is understanding.

This quality is not so much an attribute of any individual teacher, but of higher consciousness itself. It is merely personified in the form of the spiritual master. But it is also the very core and essence of your own being, could you but see into yourself deeply enough. Then you would realize that all of what you thought were incompetencies, bad deeds and harmful thoughts and acts were merely pàrt of your evolutionary process, of learning from those mistakes to understand yourself and others more and more completely. As you grow and your enlightenment unfolds, all of these are left behind and you abide in the joy and harmony that comes with love and forgiveness.

Love is the fountainhead of the perennial stream of life that flows from eternity to eternity and forgiveness is the inner strength that is cultivated in the path of enlightenment. The great people live in the world by being aware of the fact that this life is like passing through one of the camps in the long journey of human destiny. They do not indulge in strengthening the thought forms of hatred, jealousy, pride and prejudice. Forgiveness is the strength that helps them in unfolding themselves and opening up to the reality.

The Authors

Swami Rama

Yogi, scientist, philosopher, humanitarian, and mystic poet, Swami Rama is the founder and spiritual head of the Himalayan International Institute of Yoga Science and Philosophy, with its headquarters in Honesdale, Pennsylvania, and therapy and educational centers throughout the world. He was born in a Himalayan valley of Uttar Pradesh, India, in 1925 and was initiated in early childhood by a great sage of the Himalayas. He studied with many adepts, and then traveled to Tibet to study with his grandmaster. From 1949 to 1952 he held the respected position of Shankaracharya (spiritual leader) in Karvirpitham in the South of India. He then returned to the Himalayas to intensify his meditative practices in the cave monasteries and to establish an ashram in Rishikesh.

Later he continued his investigation of Western psychology and philosophy at several European universities, and he taught in Japan before coming to the United States in 1969. The following year he served as a consultant to the Voluntary Controls Project of the Research Department of the Menninger Foundation. There he demonstrated, under laboratory conditions, precise control over his autonomic nervous system and brain. The findings of that research increased the scientific community's understanding of the human ability to control autonomic functioning and to attain previously unrecognized levels of consciousness.

In 1971 Swami Rama founded the Himalayan Institute as a means to synthesize the ancient teachings of the East with the modern approaches of the West. He has played a major role in bringing the insights of yoga psychology and philosophy to the attention of the physicians and psychologists of the West. He is the author of numerous books published by the Himalayan Institute.

In 1990 Swami Rama founded the Himalayan Institute Charitable Hospital Trust in India. This project is designed to serve the people of the Himalayan foothills with a modern hospital, medical education institution, and research facility. The mission of the Hospital Trust is to develop integrated, cost-effective approaches to health care that address the needs of the local people and can also serve as a resource-appropriate model for under-served populations worldwide.

Swami Rama currently spends most of his time in the mountains of northern India. He continues to teach students from around the world while intensifying his writing and meditative practices.

Swami Ajaya, Ph.D.

Swami Ajaya has practiced clinical psychology for over twenty years and has acted as a consultant to several mental health centers. He was educated at Wesleyan University and the University of California at Berkeley. After serving as a postdoctoral fellow at the University of Wisconsin Department of Psychiatry and teaching at the University, he traveled and studied with various sages of India, being ordained a monk by Swami Rama. Swami Ajaya is the author of *Psychotherapy East and West: A Unifying Paradigm* and *Yoga Psychology,* and a co-author of *Yoga and Psychotherapy.*

The main building of the national headquarters, Honesdale, Pa.

The Himalayan Institute

Since its establishment in 1971, the Himalayan Institute has been dedicated to helping individuals develop themselves physically, mentally, and spiritually, as well as contributing to the transformation of society. All the Institute programs—educational, therapeutic, research—emphasize holistic health, yoga, and meditation as tools to help achieve those goals. Institute programs combine the best of ancient wisdom and modern science, of Eastern teachings and Western technologies. We invite you to join with us in this ongoing process of personal growth and development.

Our beautiful national headquarters, on a wooded 400-acre campus in the Pocono Mountains of northeastern Pennsylvania, provides a peaceful, healthy setting for our seminars, classes, and training programs in the principles and practices of holistic living. Students from around the world have joined us here to attend programs in such diverse areas as biofeedback and stress reduction, hatha yoga, meditation, diet and nutrition, philosophy and metaphysics, and practical psychology for better living. We see the realization of our human potentials as a lifelong quest, leading to increased health, creativity, happiness, awareness, and improving the quality of life.

The Institute is a nonprofit organization. Your membership in the Institute helps to support its programs. Please call or write for information on becoming a member.

Institute Programs, Services, and Facilities

All Institute programs share an emphasis on conscious, holistic living and personal self-development. You may enjoy any of a number of diverse programs, including:

• Special weekend or extended seminars to teach skills and techniques for increasing your ability to be healthy and enjoy life
• Holistic health services
• Professional training for health professionals
• Meditation retreats and advanced meditation instruction
• Cooking and nutritional training
• Hatha yoga and exercise workshops
• Residential programs for self-development

The Himalayan Institute Charitable Hospital

A major aspect of the Institute's work around the world is its support of the construction and management of a modern, comprehensive hospital and holistic health facility in the mountain area of Dehra Dun, India. Outpatient facilities are already providing medical care to those in need, and mobile units have been equipped to visit outlying villages. Construction work on the main hospital building is progressing as scheduled.

We welcome financial support to help with the construction and the provision of services. We also welcome donations of medical supplies, equipment, or professional expertise. If you would like further information on the Hospital, please contact us.

Himalayan Institute Publications

Art of Joyful Living	Swami Rama
Book of Wisdom (Ishopanishad)	Swami Rama
A Call to Humanity	Swami Rama
Celestial Song/Gobind Geet	Swami Rama
Choosing a Path	Swami Rama
The Cosmic Drama: Bichitra Natak	Swami Rama
Enlightenment Without God	Swami Rama
Exercise Without Movement	Swami Rama
Freedom from the Bondage of Karma	Swami Rama
Indian Music, Volume I	Swami Rama
Inspired Thoughts of Swami Rama	Swami Rama
Japji: Meditation in Sikhism	Swami Rama
Lectures on Yoga	Swami Rama
Life Here and Hereafter	Swami Rama
Living with the Himalayan Masters	Swami Rama
Love and Family Life	Swami Rama
Love Whispers	Swami Rama
Meditation and Its Practice	Swami Rama
Nitnem	Swami Rama
Path of Fire and Light, Vol. I	Swami Rama
Path of Fire and Light, Vol. II	Swami Rama
Perennial Psychology of the Bhagavad Gita	Swami Rama
A Practical Guide to Holistic Health	Swami Rama
Sukhamani Sahib: Fountain of Eternal Joy	Swami Rama
The Valmiki Ramayana Retold in Verse	Swami Rama
The Wisdom of the Ancient Sages	Swami Rama
Creative Use of Emotion	Swami Rama, Swami Ajaya
Science of Breath	Swami Rama, Rudolph Ballentine, M.D., Alan Hymes, M.D.
Yoga and Psychotherapy	Swami Rama, Rudolph Ballentine, M.D., Swami Ajaya, Ph.D.
The Mystical Poems of Kabir	Swami Rama, Robert Regli
Yoga-sutras of Patanjali	Usharbudh Arya, D.Litt.
Superconscious Meditation	Usharbudh Arya, D.Litt.
Mantra and Meditation	Usharbudh Arya, D.Litt.
Philosophy of Hatha Yoga	Usharbudh Arya, D.Litt.
Meditation and the Art of Dying	Usharbudh Arya, D.Litt.
God	Usharbudh Arya, D.Litt.
Psychotherapy East and West	Swami Ajaya, Ph.D.
Yoga Psychology	Swami Ajaya, Ph.D.
Diet and Nutrition	Rudolph Ballentine, M.D.
Joints and Glands Exercises	Rudolph Ballentine, M.D. (ed.)
Transition to Vegetarianism	Rudolph Ballentine, M.D.
Theory and Practice of Meditation	Rudolph Ballentine, M.D. (ed.)
Freedom from Stress	Phil Nuernberger, Ph.D.

Homeopathic Remedies	Dale Buegel, M.D., Blair Lewis, P.A.-C, Dennis Chernin, M.D., M.P.H.
Hatha Yoga Manual I	Samskrti and Veda
Hatha Yoga Manual II	Samskrti and Judith Franks
Seven Systems of Indian Philosophy	Rajmani Tigunait, Ph.D.
Shakti Sadhana: Steps to Samadhi	Rajmani Tigunait, Ph.D.
The Tradition of the Himalayan Masters	Rajmani Tigunait, Ph.D.
Yoga on War and Peace	Rajmani Tigunait, Ph.D.
Swami	Doug Boyd
Sikh Gurus	K.S. Duggal
Philosophy and Faith of Sikhism	K.S. Duggal
The Quiet Mind	John Harvey, Ph.D. (ed.)
Himalayan Mountain Cookery	Martha Ballentine
The Man Who Never Died	Dr. Gopal Singh
Yogasana for Health	Yogiraj Behramji
Meditation in Christianity	Himalayan Institute
Spiritual Journal	Himalayan Institute
Blank Books	Himalayan Institute

To order or to request a free mail order catalog call or write
The Himalayan Publishers
RR 1, Box 405
Honesdale, PA 18431
Toll-free 1-800-822-4547